The Survival Guide To SaaS Optimization

Jim Hussey

ISBN 978-1-950647-81-1

Cover background copyright Can Stock Photo / Andrey Kuzmin

Publisher's Cataloging-in-Publication data

Names: Hussey, James M., author.
Title: The survival guide to SaaS optimization : a practical guide to SaaS
governance & optimization best practices / Jim Hussey.
Description: Lakewood, CO; James M. Hussey, 2021.
Identifiers: ISBN: 978-1-950647-81-1
Subjects: LCSH Cloud computing. | Computer software. | Application software. |
Software engineering--Management. | Agile software development. | Information
technology--Management. | Business enterprises--Computer networks--
Management. | BISAC BUSINESS & ECONOMICS / Information Management |
COMPUTERS / Information Technology
Classification: LCC HD30.37 .H87 2021 | DDC 004.36--dc23

Publishing assistance by BookCrafters, Parker, Colorado.
www.bookcrafters.net

Table of Contents

Introduction

Hello and welcome to *The Survival Guide to SaaS Optimization*. Thank you for your investment in time and resources! My goal is to provide you outstanding value to help you achieve enhanced results in your endeavor to effectively govern and manage your organizations SaaS portfolio.

The pages that follow feature the strategies, tactics and templates of the Empowered SaaS Optimization (ESO) framework. This framework features 9 tools that will help reinforce the principles in a clean, concise format that you will be able to put to immediate use. Much like my previous book *The SAM Leader Survival Guide* which featured the SAM Empowerment Framework (SEF), I combine my personal corporate experience when I was tasked to develop my organizations internal policies and onboarding practices for SaaS providers with over a dozen interviews with executives responsible for their organizations SaaS governance. In addition, I have spoken with multiple CEO's of the firms actively marketing SaaS Optimization and Management platforms to gain their insight and observations on trends and emerging best practices.

These discussions confirmed that what I had experienced in my corporate role is occurring on a broader scale. Achieving effective SaaS governance and optimization requires collaboration across multiple functional areas to deliver the end-to-end diligence required. In addition to Sourcing, SaaS optimization requires the active involvement of Technology Vendor Management, Software Asset Management, Information Security, Third Party Risk Management, Governance, Risk & Compliance, IT Finance and others. Organizations are just now beginning to look at how to best coordinate an approach to reduce widespread value leakage while closely monitoring potential operational risk.

The Survival Guide to SaaS Optimization represents the culmination of this research, putting forward the best practices identified in the form of the Empowered SaaS Optimization framework. The ESO framework 9 unique tools will guide SaaS professionals tasked with developing their organizations SaaS governance and optimization capability through a logical progression of steps and activities to determine SaaS segmentation, appropriate policies and controls, process alignment, clarity of SaaS roles and responsibilities, risk-based categorization, risk-based categorization and ultimately and ultimately the multi-dimensional, multi-level activities to deliver truly empowered SaaS optimization.

Once again thank you for spending this time with me and I look forward to enriching your career and capabilities to deliver meaningful results and value to your organizations SaaS partners.

Jim Hussey

Author – The Survival Guide to SaaS Optimization

Creator – Empowered SaaS Optimization Framework

Acknowledgment

2020 is certainly a year none of us will forget. In many ways we all had to learn new ways to perform our core task as employees, parents and friends to stay connected and somehow maintain a small level of normalcy.

As I sent off my previous book *The SAM Leader Survival Guide* for final edit and formatting with the publisher, I took one last review of my interview notes and noticed a surprising gap. In all the SAM leaders I interviewed, despite my questions pertaining to SaaS, few indicated any engagement or focus on this area. How can such a high-growth, visible form of cloud services not be a top priority on the SAM agenda?

With this question posed, my journey to development of *The Survival Guide to SaaS Optimization* had begun!

To all the 12 individuals I interviewed representing the multiple disciplines impacted by SaaS services I thank you. To the executives I interviewed at leading and emerging SaaS Management Platform providers, your insight was invaluable. To the leading researchers and content managers at the associations and consultancies serving this community, I thank you for your open and direct input. When blended with my personal corporate experience concerning SaaS governance, these multiple perspectives ultimately led to creation of the Empowered SaaS Optimization framework.

Lastly, I want to thank my wife Kim for her unyielding support. As always, she was a great sounding board and challenged many of the principles, forcing me to focus and ensure each item produced the intended value. While she is my toughest critic, she is my greatest confidant and asset.

Welcome

Little did I know the series of events a simple, casual lunch was to set-off. I was meeting my good friend for a lunch in our corporate cafeteria. My buddy was the Sourcing Director for the IT Category and I was Vice President of Technology Vendor Management. We met frequently over lunch to share the issues and challenges we were experiencing in order to maintain close coordination as we attempted to effectively govern an annual global IT spend that exceeded $800 million.

On this particular day, my buddy was very preoccupied. When I asked what was on his mind, he shared with me that he had just left a meeting with the Chief Financial Officer and the Chief Procurement Officer during which the issue of Software as a Service was raised and the apparent lack of controls. It appeared that the Chief Compliance Officer had been informed by regulators of a judgement due to a rogue marketing program utilizing a SaaS application at one of our global locations. Sensitive customer data was outside approved protections and required locations, producing a significant potential fine.

This simple conversation, and the supporting activities I jointly developed with my Sourcing partner, has ultimately led to we writing this book and developing the Empowered SaaS Optimization (ESO) framework you hold in your hands. Over the past 4 years, I have refined the strategies and tactics used to enable organizations implement successful SaaS governance and optimization operations which now represent a portfolio of 9 targeted tools. The ESO framework, when applied in the proper sequence and used to facilitate collaboration across the multi-functional team we are about to define, has helped dozens of organizations achieve outstanding SaaS governance and optimization results.

The Survival Guide to SaaS Optimization and the ESO framework represents the blending of my personal experience establishing a SaaS governance and optimization function for my organization, my advisory support helping clients design and implement a solution appropriate for their company, 12 separate interviews with executives on the emerging subject of challenges and opportunities presented by SaaS capabilities to their organizations as well as multiple discussions with CEO's of SaaS Management Platform providers.

Throughout these discussions, I observed that there is no central, primary point of contact who evaluates, purchased, implements and governs SaaS partners. IT Vendor Management, IT Finance, Sourcing leaders, InfoSec leaders, and Compliance leaders (Third Party Risk Management and Governance, Risk & Compliance) ALL have interest in establishing effective governance and optimization practices for SaaS assets. Yet no single individual outright owns the agenda.

Based on this insight, *The Survival Guide to SaaS Optimization* has been developed to help Sourcing, IT Finance, IT operations, InfoSec, SAM Professionals, Third Party Risk Management (TPRM), Compliance, Business Unit and IT leaders apply the Empowered SaaS Optimization (ESO) framework to achieve outstanding SaaS optimization results. In fact, The Empowered SaaS Optimization (ESO) framework blends a cross-functional approach, combining components from each discipline providing familiarity to those involved with SaaS governance responsibility regardless of functional role. There are elements that will be familiar to Technology Vendor Managers, Third Party Risk Management, Sourcing, IT, IT Finance, Information Security and Software Asset Management. It is the blending of these skills and perspectives that establishes the comprehensive strategy and tactics necessary to achieve true governance and optimization of an organizations SaaS partners, establishing the path to a dedicated SaaS Optimization Office (SOO).

Based on the increased visibility of SaaS with corporate executives, the rapidly growing level of spend and expanding services being delivered in the SaaS model, *The Survival Guide to SaaS Optimization* has begun to observe organizations interest in establishing a more definitive way to manage their portfolio of SaaS services. Currently there appears to be two primary approaches:

- Sourcing and other interested leaders bring together a group of functional representatives to form an ongoing team to collaborate on SaaS governance and optimization best practices. *The Survival Guide to SaaS Optimization* refers to this approach as the SaaS Governance Team (SGT).

- When an organization's executive team views the level of SaaS spend as an opportunity to manage efficiency, a potential threat to regulatory compliance or increases operational vulnerabilities, an executive sponsor is assigned and tasked with establishing a dedicated function. *The Survival Guide to SaaS Optimization* refers to an organizations decision to hire dedicated professionals to own the agenda for driving SaaS governance and optimization as the SaaS Optimization Office (SOO).

Without realizing it, during my fateful lunch meeting, I agreed to join forces with my IT Sourcing partner and we assumed the role of what I now call the 'SaaS Governance Enablers'. I suspect if you are reading these words, you will shortly come to identify yourself as the SaaS Governance Enabler within your organization! The following pages are filled with detailed guidance and the tools necessary for you to be an early mover in the SaaS governance and optimization segment and position yourself as a leader in this high growth segment.

The SaaS Optimization Challenge

Setting the Stage

There are many sources of information covering Software as a Service (SaaS) market dynamics including respected consultancies, SaaS platform providers and other SaaS luminaries, all pointing to the tremendous growth cloud computing has had the past 15 years. It is too early to tell the true impact COVID-19 will have on these estimates and forecast, but one thing appears to be certain, SaaS growth has not slowed and there is high potential growth has accelerated.

The Survival Guide to SaaS Optimization will focus exclusively on SaaS dynamics, challenges and emerging best practices for the benefit of SaaS Governance Enablers. I do not intend to communicate that Infrastructure as a Service (IaaS) and Platform as a Service (PaaS) are less important, but I have found identification, selection, implementation and management activities for SaaS differ significantly than the other cloud options as they remain largely controlled by Information Technology. While this may change as those services evolve, SaaS today evokes strong emotions regarding shadow IT and business operations independently going out and purchasing SaaS capabilities. This dynamic creates the potential for increased Information Security vulnerabilities, General Data Protection Regulation (GDPR) regulatory exposure and additional risk due to poorly communicated and enforced SaaS policies and controls.

Leading IT consulting firm Gartner projects global SaaS revenue to reach the $98 billion mark by the end of 2020 and a forecasted 18% increase in 2021, bringing global SaaS spend to $113 billion by the end of 2021. These forecasts are pre-COVID-19 so it will be interesting to see if this is maintained or potentially accelerates due to the dramatic shift to adoption of a remote workforce and the necessary services to enable this model.

Gartner also estimates that between 2017-2022 enterprise software will have an overall growth rate of +175% with SaaS estimated to experience a growth rate during this period of +241%, trailing only Public Cloud (IaaS/PaaS) which is estimated to have a +358% growth during this same period.

It is the opinion of *The Survival Guide to SaaS Optimization* that Gartner's estimates, while they may appear dramatic, may in fact underestimate SaaS market growth. We are poised for continued focus and investment from enterprise software publishers including SAP, Oracle, Microsoft, Google, VMWare and others in transitioning to the SaaS model. The manner Wall St. is rewarding valuations has clearly shown the investment communities comfort with the SaaS model and the positive bottom-line impact for Independent Software Vendors (ISV's).

About The Survival Guide to SaaS Optimization

This book has been developed and structured as a reference guide, providing SaaS Governance Enablers a step-by-step guide to establish a dedicated SaaS Optimization Office. While you can tell the approach and style is conversational, I have attempted to structure the content in an easy-to-follow, logical sequence to enable quick identification of information to help you with the specific item you are dealing with. *The Survival Guide to SaaS Optimization* supports this content with the Empowered SaaS Optimization (ESO) framework which provides specific tools and templates throughout the book to provide visuals so you can utilize the recommended actions to the fullest extent possible.

The Survival Guide to SaaS Optimization is structured in the following 5 core parts with the content delivered in the logical sequence I have observed most effective time and time again with clients.

- **Part 1 – SaaS Governance:** This is the critical first step for organizations to address in order to establish the framework necessary to achieve truly Empowered SaaS Optimization.

Part 1 will discuss the importance to view SaaS as a large, global market requiring careful consideration of the segments and categories that have emerged, the challenges and opportunities to govern SaaS across the SaaS life cycle and assign the appropriate task of the cross-functional SaaS team to establish end to end governance.

- **Part 2 – SaaS Optimization:** Building upon the concepts and recommendations of SaaS Governance, Part 2 decomposes SaaS Optimization into the multiple characteristics that need to be addressed in order to true multi-level optimization. This analysis is a risk-based assessment that enables an organization to carefully monitor those partners that present the best opportunities for innovation and competitive advantage while continually monitoring emerging risk and potential operational disruption.

- **Part 3 – The Case for the SaaS Optimization Office:** It is the opinion of *The Survival Guide to SaaS Optimization* that organizations need to explore establishing a dedicated function to govern and maintain optimized SaaS partnerships. Part 3, The Case for the SaaS Optimization Office, explores the benefit of this emerging trend and the evolutionary path organizations are implementing today to plant the seed for SaaS governance. With the initiative of a few key operational leaders, which I refer to as the SaaS Governance Enablers, an internal team of cross-functional members is identified to provide guidance and recommendations for effective SaaS governance and optimization. I refer to this as the SaaS Governance Team (SGT). Once established and productive, organizations move to the next stage with a decision to fund a dedicated SaaS operation. At this point, the SaaS governance capability is referred to as the SaaS Optimization Office (SOO).

- **Part 4 – SaaS Optimization Office Executive Alignment:** There are multiple proven activities any organization needs to establish in order to gain alignment across sponsors, stakeholders and operations. Due to the involvement of business unit leadership in the identification and selection of SaaS capabilities, these tactics are invaluable for SaaS Governance Enablers to gain the required support and alignment.

- **Part 5 – ESO Framework Methodology Implementation:** The 5th and final section of *The Survival Guide to SaaS Optimization* provides practical guidance for SaaS Governance Enablers to apply the Empowered SaaS Optimization framework. Drawing on my experience supporting multiple organizations successfully implement SaaS governance capabilities, this section is a 'how to succeed' and create an effective SaaS governance operation.

ESO Framework Tool Overview

I would like to take a moment to provide background on the Empowered SaaS Optimization framework. The 9 tools that are provided in *The Survival Guide to SaaS Optimization* have been included to help you visualize how you can best apply the strategy and tactics being described. In total, the ESO framework provides a step-by-step guide for SaaS Governance Enablers to establish the focus necessary to socialize the importance of SaaS governance and create the transparency necessary to generate executive awareness of the benefit a formal SaaS governance and optimization effort will deliver. I have had the opportunity to utilize this framework multiple times and am pleased to say the simplicity of the approach has delivered outstanding results. This book will provide you the guidance and coaching necessary to successfully utilize and implement the ESO framework.

Empowered SaaS Optimization (ESO) Framework Tools

- Tool 1: SaaS Active Universe Roster (Page 27)

- Tool 2: SaaS Control Map (Page 31)

- Tool 3: SaaS Governance Framework (Page 48)

- Tool 4: SaaS Optimization Decomposition (Page 68)

- Tool 5: SaaS Partner Risk Categorization (Page 74)

- Tool 6: SaaS Optimization Levers (Page 80)

- Tool 7: SOO Mission Statement (Page 113)

- Tool 8: SOO Value Statement (Page 114)

- Tool 9: SaaS Governance & Optimization Maturation Map (Page 131)

Part 1 – SaaS Governance

I know many of you are asking yourself 'I want to know about SaaS optimization, why are we wasting our time on governance?' Gartner estimates that 30% of all funds invested in SaaS applications is wasted due to poor governance practices. Labeling this wasted investment as 'Toxic Spend', organizations are rushing to develop strategies and tactics to optimize with little understanding of the multi-level complexities.

To fully understand the extent of potential SaaS optimization within your organization, I urge you to work through this section as it will form a powerful foundation for you and your team to achieve outstanding SaaS governance and optimization results. The governance activities we are about to review establish a risk-based approach to the subject of governing and optimizing your organizations SaaS portfolio. For those of you in heavily regulated industries, you will see the subtle alignment with Third Party Risk Management (TPRM) and Governance, Risk and Compliance (GRC) practices. For those of you with firms placing a heavy emphasis on Information Security, you will see the aspect of monitoring vulnerabilities. For those of you who are not in these market segments, you will be able to broaden your communication with the 'C-Suite' in terms dominating today's Board discussions: Business resilience, risk monitoring, ongoing optimization and continual identification of alternatives for rapid transition and transformation.

When I am running a training session on SaaS optimization or working with IT, Sourcing or Compliance executives frustrated by their inability to control their growing SaaS footprint, I ask them a basic question: 'Can you truly optimize what is not governed?' Many times, I encounter the reaction I just described where they only want to focus on optimization. However, after a few moments and sharing the overview of how a comprehensive governance model is key to achieve true optimization, these executives settle down and are ready to engage on the subject.

Now that we have set the stage for a focused discussion on SaaS governance, let's dig into the tactics and activities that will enable your organization to reduce risk associated with SaaS-sprawl across the enterprise, maintain diligence on usage and drive maximum value from those SaaS partners identified as strategic to your business.

The Trigger: SaaS Governance Enabler

The challenge of governing SaaS partners is experienced across many functional areas and disciplines within an organization. Typically, it will be the Chief Procurement Officer (CPO) or head of sourcing that brings visibility to the issue, but it takes multiple teams to join in before the concept of a focused concerted effort to achieve SaaS governance and optimization gains traction. If you are reading this book, I suspect you either already have involvement or responsibility to govern and optimize your organizations SaaS portfolio of partners or you are concerned about this area and are looking to get some practical advice on how to implement SaaS optimization best practices. Regardless of where you are on your SaaS journey, *The Survival Guide to SaaS Optimization* and the ESO framework will provide practical guidance that can be put to use immediately.

If you are in the position where you believe your organization needs to establish a more formal focus on SaaS but none exist as yet, I highly recommend you work across your organization to find others of the same opinion who will support the effort to create a greater emphasis on SaaS governance. In my conversations with executives from the SaaS Management Platform firms, they shared that the corporate leaders who reach out to them on the issue of SaaS optimization tend to be from Sourcing, Compliance, Information Security (InfoSec), Vendor Management and IT Finance. In my case, I was approached by the IT Sourcing Category Manager on the need to establish policies and controls for SaaS services. Without realizing it at the time, we were acting as what I now call as 'SaaS

Governance Enablers'; those individuals who assume the role to trigger greater focus on the challenges to govern SaaS assets.

As SaaS Governance Enablers, we jointly pushed the SaaS governance agenda and were successful in getting the support of the Chief of Compliance and the CFO. Their support helped us to gain sponsorship for a team of functional experts to come together for the purpose of designing SaaS onboarding requirements. This team, which we labeled the SaaS Governance Team, included representation from InfoSec, IT Finance and Compliance. When combined with executive messaging from the CFO, our task force was successful at establishing SaaS policies and controls across our organizations global footprint.

Use of a SaaS service by a business unit or functional team can be a highly political challenge for a central souring or IT function to influence. Gaining sponsorship from executives whose roles cut across all business units and functions such as the CFO, Chief Compliance Officer (CCO) or Chief Information Security Officer (CISO) helps raise the importance of SaaS governance and optimization above potential individual interest.

With SaaS governance and optimization receiving clear executive endorsement, the next key step is to establish an ongoing team of functional leaders to create a comprehensive definition of SaaS governance.

The Base: SaaS Governance Team

As we move deeper into the subject and discipline of SaaS governance, it is important to establish a mindset that SaaS impacts multiple units and functions across an organization. While the issues and concerns may be very different, there is tremendous benefit when an organization assembles a team of individuals representing multiple disciplines to create a single unified view of SaaS governance needs. By doing so, the view of SaaS governance is broadened, representing a comprehensive view of the opportunities and challenges; setting the stage for an organization-wide SaaS vision.

The Survival Guide to SaaS Optimization believes one of the most significant challenges facing organizations today when it comes to the opportunity to achieve greater value for their SaaS investment is the silo'd and federated manner in which the subject is currently treated. As I work across a client's leadership team, I am always amazed to see how many are truly concerned with the runaway use of SaaS applications. While seeing the challenge and potential risk, each leader views this exposure from their unique perspective. When I bring them together for a focused conversation on SaaS governance and optimization, these leaders invariably share their specific concerns and a comprehensive plan takes shape.

As the SaaS Governance Enabler, you have the opportunity to drive this activity using the ESO framework. However, before doing so, I wanted to share with you my general observations from the following functional areas who will be key for you to secure their participation and support. While every organization is different and may feature functions with more political capital than others, when the subject of SaaS surfaces, I have found the following high-level concerns or frustrations related to SaaS governance and optimization:

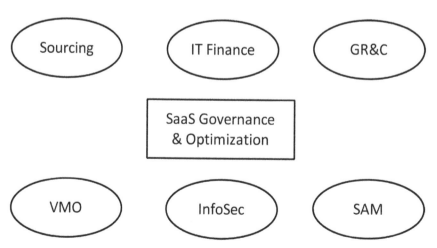

Figure 1 – SaaS-Sensitive Functional Areas

- Sourcing

  o How are we going to maintain diligence to optimize renewals? How do we access usage data to harvest license levels and types ongoing? What are the terms prominent in the SaaS market today?

- IT Finance

  o How do I maintain an accurate accounting of SaaS spend? How will we budget, track cost and assign to the appropriate cost center? How do I track rogue individual or business unit SaaS purchases?

- Governance, Risk & Compliance / TPRM

  o How do we document the process by which we assess, score and monitored risk to satisfy regulatory investigations?

- Vendor Management

  o How do we measure service level performance and what is the recourse for service breach? How do we track the Deliverables and Obligations stated in the agreement?

- Information Security

  o How do we control vulnerabilities and ensure the SaaS providers meet and maintain our InfoSec requirements?

- Software Asset Management

  o How do we extract the required usage data for optimization? What are the compliance implications?

This is just a short sampling of questions being asked across an enterprise today. With executive sponsorship established, the goal of the SaaS Governance Enabler is to bring functional representation from these areas together to perform as a SaaS Governance Team (SGT): a cross-functional team of professionals coming together for the single purpose of establishing effective SaaS Governance and Optimization practices.

With any team, there is an individual or group that needs to take action and initiate the discussion regarding SaaS governance. *The Survival Guide to SaaS Optimization* believes the leader of Sourcing, perhaps in collaboration with Vendor Management, Third Party Risk Management (TPRM) or Compliance, is in the best position to push the SaaS governance agenda, assuming the SaaS Governance Enabler role. Sourcing leaders were successful with executives to establish important governance capabilities in the areas of IT offshore outsourcing or Telecommunications Expense Management (TEM). They now have the opportunity to stress the importance of establishing critical 'pre-signature' activities for SaaS services as well as communicate the need for 'post-signature' governance of SaaS services and partners.

The Structure: SaaS Optimization Office

With strong executive sponsorship secured and agreement to fund a dedicated, SaaS governance and optimization team, the SaaS Optimization Office (SOO) is established. The goal of this team is to continually deliver savings and cost avoidance through expert SaaS license management while monitoring potential risk and security vulnerabilities. As SaaS applications continue to be integrated into core business processes, the SOO will grow in importance.

Before we move off this subject, it is important to note what will be addressed later in *The Survival Guide to SaaS Optimization*. In my experience working with multiple global clients, I continually observer the emergence of SaaS governance and optimization as a corporate agenda is most effective when sponsored by an organization's senior most finance executive. The Chief Financial Officer (CFO) has the ability to transcend political lines and business unit silos to drive the required visibility and accountability to establish effective SaaS governance and optimization policies. An emerging executive role that can bring equal political clout to the need for SaaS governance is the Chief Compliance Officer (CCO) or head of Governance, Risk & Compliance (GRC) function. As executives becomes more aware utilization of SaaS services can expose organizations to mismanagement of data, privacy and regulatory judgements, I anticipate Compliance leadership will become strong advocates for implementation of greater SaaS controls and ongoing due diligence.

What this leads to is the realization that an organization approach to SaaS governance and optimization will need to evolve and mature as the level of spend, potential risk exposure and environment vulnerabilities from these services grows.

SaaS Market Overview

It is well documented the use of SaaS offerings has taken firm hold in global enterprises of all sizes. The ability to move rapidly from identification of a need to selection, deployment and implementation of a SaaS capability is unchallenged. However, this ability to move quickly does not come without risk and in some cases, significant operational damage can occur.

SaaS Growth

We have previously shared Gartner's forecast for the continued use and expansion of SaaS offerings across a dizzying range of disciplines and this does not appear to be slowing anytime soon. SaaS providers have targeted all potential areas to provide their capabilities covering historical legacy applications and environments across to emerging, new breed capabilities incorporating Intelligent Automation (IA) combined with powerful analytics. In fact, private equity firms and venture capital funds are pushing 'SaaS-first' market strategies for their software publisher portfolio firms.

It is easy to see the rational:

- Customizations and configurations are the client's responsibility

- Centralized feature 'push' enables easy and consistent client management

- Clients own management of license and user metric responsibility

- Service Levels are more easily maintained and less stringent than on-premise requirements

- Lower maintenance cost due to removal of back-version management

- Higher margin / Higher valuations

- Easier and more rapid sales cycle due to multiple potential buyers removed from central Sourcing experts or Information Technology

In short, SaaS appears to have been endorsed as the optimal adoption of cloud services by organizations and the preferred manner for Independent Software Vendors (ISVs) to deliver capability. *The Survival Guide to SaaS Optimization* and the Empowered SaaS Optimization framework has been designed to provide organizations best practices to govern and optimize their growing portfolio of SaaS services and applications.

SaaS Diversity

While technology is evolving rapidly, SaaS offerings and services have enjoyed meteoric growth and I believe are on the doorsteps for dramatic growth that will broaden and deepen SaaS penetration within global enterprises. Longstanding enterprise software publishers are rapidly reengineering their core offerings with next generation SaaS delivery models. This dynamic, combined with the broad, overall growth of new, task specific ISV's, promise to make the field SaaS services applications incredibly diverse. Organizations must take steps in order to understand the relative importance and classification of the expanding SaaS universe in their environment.

The first and most basic action for SaaS Governance Enablers is to understand it is no longer sufficient to label a service or application as SaaS. To develop the required governance and optimization strategies and tactics, organizations must establish clear SaaS segmentation categories to determine the level of diligence required to effectively govern and optimize each unique segment.

SaaS Segmentation

Despite the meteoric growth and expansion of the SaaS market, most consultants still refer to this +$100 Billion market as a single generic group of SaaS services. I have found this view of SaaS to be very dangerous for organizations as it ignores the nuances and unique aspects of each specific SaaS offering. Managing services such as Human Capital Management (HCM) SaaS capabilities from Workday and SuccessFactors with the same level of diligence and monitoring as a project management module being used by a small team in a far-off business unit makes little sense.

The truth is not all SaaS services are equal and organizations, as well as the consulting and platform providers focusing on this community, need to recognize the multi-dimensional, multi-faceted nature of the SaaS market or run the risk of applying a generic approach to governance and optimization of these partners. Missing the real value to be gained by optimal use of these SaaS capabilities and ignoring potential regulatory and compliance risk and information security vulnerabilities these services can create.

The first critical element of the Empowered SaaS Optimization (ESO) framework is for SaaS Governance Enablers and members of the SaaS Governance Team to come together and begin the process of defining the relevant SaaS segments currently in the corporate environment in order to structure and prioritize SaaS governance and optimization activities.

- **Benefits of SaaS Segmentation:** As we move deeper into SaaS Segmentation, a few key themes will emerge that support effective implementation of a company-wide SaaS governance and optimization framework. These themes enable the extended enterprise to quickly assess and assign the segment for an identified SaaS application as well as identify areas that may prove problematic based on the pre-defined criteria. Development of a SaaS Segmentation structure answers the critical questions concerning policy, controls, approvals, evaluation criteria, potential exposure and other important requirements intended to protect the organization. Combined with clear consequence in the event of non-compliance, assigning a SaaS segment to current and potential new partners establishes the discipline and consistency necessary for rapid and effective identification of those SaaS capabilities and applications requiring additional monitoring and diligence in addition to optimization activities.

- **SaaS Segmentation Groupings:** Ultimately how SaaS segments are defined and structured will be unique to your organization. As previously stated, the SaaS Governance Team (SGT) is composed of an effective cross-section of disciplines. Utilizing this team in a collaborative, workshop setting to define the number and type of segments within your organization and the specific characteristics of each is a powerful first step to creating the SaaS governance framework. During this process, SaaS Governance Enablers need to ensure each member of the team is contributing and facilitate discussion so each member is able to voice their unique requirements.

The Survival Guide to SaaS Optimization offers the following generic SaaS Segments as I have consistently observed these groupings when working with clients. SaaS Governance Enablers should utilize the opportunity to discuss SaaS segmentation to gain insight to the perspective of executive sponsors and stakeholders as this will be an indication of their understanding of the current SaaS environment. As the SaaS Governance Team then works through the process of assigning SaaS applications to specific segment, I always find there is a level of surprise with the final outcome with certain segments having significantly more representation than anticipated. Many times, indicating a level of risk and vulnerabilities not previously perceived.

- **Enterprise SaaS:** Assigned partners to the 'Enterprise SaaS' segment will represent a small percent of an organization's overall portfolio of SaaS partners. However, despite the relatively small universe of firms in this category, the level of spend in this category is growing dramatically. Much of this is due to the fact Enterprise SaaS offerings are essentially re-architected on-premises solutions on which core business functions are built and integrated deeply to corporate value and supply chains.

  The Enterprise SaaS category is currently dominated by Microsoft's family of O365 products, Salesforce, ServiceNow, Adobe's CreativeCloud, SAP's Success Factors and Workday to name a few. Oracle and SAP have aggressive growth plans moving to subscription-based models. These are the capabilities critical to business operations.

  In addition to these major enterprise players, there are numerous SaaS pureplay providers who have quickly established their capabilities as corporate standard or expanded their modules to provide ever expanding services. I see Zoom, Slack, BOX and others that have moved quickly from an individual or workgroup purchase decision to an enterprise buy. There will be more to follow!

- **Industry Specific SaaS:** While we may measure the Enterprise SaaS community in the dozens of firms, when we shift to the area of Industry Specific SaaS offerings, the list expands to hundreds that could fit this definition. Fortunately, the typical business operation will require one of these solutions to function as an enterprise platform for their specific industry. These implementations will be crucial to business operations and will require significant governance in order to maintain clarity of business solvency or emerging risk.

- **Hybrid SaaS:** This is a very interesting SaaS segment. As traditional Independent Software Vendors (ISV) rearchitect and move their offerings to subscription models, they will tend to do so moving module by module. Meaning many customers may have components of their software on-premise, perpetual licenses and other portions in the SaaS model. Requiring consistent monitoring of compliance while attempting to define optimization.

  As time progresses, this category is expected to expand followed by contraction as ISV's become predominantly SaaS based in their offerings and agreements. However, during this window, Hybrid SaaS presents a unique, multi-level challenge.

- **Human Capital Management SaaS:** *The Survival Guide to SaaS Optimization* has identified the SaaS category of Human Capital Management as an important example of a functional SaaS capability that transcends other functional SaaS offerings to behave more like an enterprise segment or hybrid segment SaaS. Due to the nature of the information and importance of well documented HR practices, *The Survival Guide to SaaS Optimization* views HCM SaaS as a separate segment but also believes due to the separation with core IT and sourcing, they represent strong optimization targets.

- **Functional SaaS:** As we move beyond enterprise, industry and hybrid SaaS segments, the number of offerings in the remaining segments grows exponentially. These tend to be the SaaS-type that shadow IT or individual business units will procure independently when a lack of policy and controls exist. Spend associated with this category can still be substantial due to the large number of providers. SaaS Governance Enablers need to apply appropriate focus to ensure privacy, risk and other key aspects are closely defined. We typically see customers place services such as File Storage & Share, training and learning management systems (LMS) and other enablers in this category.

- **Operational/Task SaaS:** There isn't a business process, sub-process or individual task that is not currently being targeted by SaaS providers. Many times, SaaS capabilities are so fine-tuned that they target an extremely narrow well-defined niche. Project management, industry specific project management, role specific project management SaaS platforms are all competing to grab their piece of the Project & Portfolio Management budget. An additional, high growth area is team collaboration platforms or business intelligence capabilities.

- **Miscellaneous:** There is no slowing of new SaaS solutions being introduced to the market. Much like the dotcom craze, Venture Capital firms are funding large portfolios of SaaS offerings as they see the combination of efficient operations and ability to control cost while driving top line revenue as highly attractive. In addition, enterprises are in the midst of a dramatic shift in software purchase patterns. Moving away from traditional, on-premise solutions to cloud offerings providing agility and easier accounting treatment.

SaaS Segmentation Outcomes

The vast majority of organizations today have limited understanding of their current total spend on SaaS capabilities or a true number of SaaS solutions and applications in their global environment. Defining SaaS segment characteristics is a first step in bringing order to this chaos. As the SaaS Governance Team identified and assigns known SaaS partners to the appropriate segment, they will begin to see if there are potential segment gaps, alignment challenges and begin to identify process challenges that may enable SaaS applications to be deployed without proper vetting. This insight will enable development of effective SaaS corporate policies and controls designed to drive consistency of evaluation requirements and criteria. *The Survival Guide to SaaS Optimization* will cover this extensively through the ESO framework.

Once the segmentation effort has been initiated and the preliminary universe of SaaS applications have been inventoried and assigned to a segment, SaaS Governance Enablers need to develop more complete profiles for the portfolio of SaaS partners. Working with sponsors, stakeholders and engaged members of the SaaS Governance Team, SaaS Governance Enablers begin the process of compiling core data points that will support analysis of SaaS category spend, effective renewal management and specify the executive sponsor for each SaaS relationship. This brings *The Survival Guide to SaaS Optimization* to the first Empowered SaaS Optimization tool, the SaaS Active Universe Roster.

SaaS Active Universe Roster

In my dealings with clients, I find many of them are challenged to truly comprehend the extent of the SaaS portfolio of services that already resides across their environment. With little understanding of the current investment in SaaS applications, renewal requirements, business unit utilization of SaaS services or who specifically is authorizing use of these services, in many respects' executives are flying blind. This lack of visibility or transparency to SaaS utilization will continue to create stress for executives as they grow increasingly anxious about potential regulatory risk exposure due to mismanagement of data, security vulnerabilities and lost value due to poor governance.

This dynamic creates a significant opportunity for SaaS Governance Enablers to step forward and bring order to this increasingly complex and diversifying environment.

Building on the initial assignment of SaaS application segment assignment, Tool 1 of the Empowered SaaS Optimization framework, the 'SaaS Active Universe Roster', is designed to capture in a single document core information regarding each identified SaaS partner and the specific SaaS application currently in use. The goal of this data gathering effort is to facilitate initiation of effective SaaS governance to help corporate executives begin to understand the on the ground reality of SaaS usage within their organization and the value to be realized by a focused, multi-discipled governance and optimization team.

SaaS Active Universe Roster Structure

The goal of producing the detailed 'SaaS Active Universe Roster' is to provide a central location for critical information regarding an organizations SaaS partners. Over time, the SaaS Active Universe Roster will serve as the baseline for all identified and documented SaaS services. Utilization of a SaaS Management Platforms discovery capability combined with alignment to additional internal process will help identify process breakdown and non-compliance gaps.

I have found that organizations will have consistent areas of interest concerning information for specific SaaS providers. The sample SaaS Active Universe Roster template offers suggested data fields that have proven successful with the majority of clients I have supported. Feel free to modify the template based on your specific needs, but do make certain to capture the executive sponsor for a SaaS application and the cost center where the cost is budgeted as this will support assigning accountability to support renewals and potential risk implications.

Empowered SaaS Optimization - Tool 1
SaaS Active Universe Roster

SaaS Partner Legal Name	SaaS Partner Product Name	SaaS Segment	Annual Spend	Initial Contract Date	Renewal Date	Renewal Frequency	Termination Notification Requirement	Executive Sponsor	Executive Sponsor Title	Internal Cost Center
<NAME>	<NAME>	Enterprise	$ -	31-Jan-20	31-Jan-23		<CONTRACT TERM>	<NAME>	<TITLE>	#
			$ -							
			$ -							
			$ -							
			$ -							
			$ -							
			$ -							
			$ -							

SaaS Active Universe Roster

- **SaaS Partner Legal Entity Name:** This is important as there is a significant amount of consolidation, failure and overall turnover in the SaaS category. Organizations need to understand the risk associated with the company behind the service and ensure entity structure is clear.

- **SaaS Product Name:** Clearly document the specific product name as well as module-level detail if applicable.

- **SaaS Segment:** Identify the SaaS Segment assigned by the SaaS Governance Team.

- **Annual Spend:** Based on contract document and additional invoices.

- **Initial Contract Date:** Length of time the SaaS capability has been in service – shows potential lost leverage

- **Renewal Date:** Identify upcoming renewal date

- **Renewal Frequency:** Many SaaS providers have frequent renewal schedules

- **Termination Notification Requirement:** Document the specific terms that govern termination of the agreement with the SaaS provider

- **Executive Sponsor:** Identify who in the organization engaged, selected and executed the agreement. This individual is the escalation point for all issues pertaining to renewal, service delivery etc. Confirm Executive sponsor alignment with the assigned cost center

- **Executive Sponsor Title:** Focused on organizational leveling to understand the level at which the SaaS service decision is being made. Is it consistent with signing authority?

- **Internal Cost Center:** Identify the specific cost center to determine budget implications and potential charge back mechanics.

The Survival Guide to SaaS Optimization identifies 11 data fields for this important, foundational report called the 'SaaS Active Universe Roster'. Some of you may see this as excessive while others may want to add several more fields. Tool 1 of the ESO framework, 'SaaS Active Universe Roster' forms the first crucial step helping organizations begin to understand their exposure and opportunities in this high growth service space. It also sets the stage for members of the SaaS Governance Team to assume more proactive involvement in the management of SaaS assets in their specific functional areas based on tangible intelligence.

SaaS Active Universe Roster Utilization

Before we move on to the next area of focus for SaaS Governance Enablers, it is important to sit back and really think about how you can leverage development of a 'SaaS Active Universe Roster' for maximum value to SaaS governance efforts. When you consider the elements suggested for the initial SaaS Active Universe Roster, a SaaS tool will help identify those SaaS applications in the environment, but the majority of the suggested fields will require 'sweat-equity' to discover the identified data. Ultimately SaaS Governance Enablers will need to investigate these additional data points to uncover the information that will form the basis of a quality SaaS governance and optimization operation.

As the team reviews the information assembled in the SaaS Active Universe Roster, SaaS Governance Enablers will begin to see potential challenges or gaps in the management of SaaS partners. These challenges can occur at any point in the relationship with the SaaS provider. It is important for SaaS Governance Enablers to overlay the 'SaaS Active Universe Roster' with the stages or phases of the SaaS lifecycle to define the foundational policies, controls, requirements and criteria by which SaaS services are to be evaluated and continually monitored. In essence creating a SaaS workflow to ensure each step and activity is successfully executed, reducing risk associated with SaaS services while optimizing spend.

The Survival Guide to SaaS Optimization refers to this detailed, multi-phase workflow as the 'SaaS Control Map'.

SaaS Control Map

Tool 2 of the Empowered SaaS Optimization framework is the SaaS Control Map. Designed to help organizations define the criteria by which a SaaS capability is monitored and controlled across the full SaaS life-cycle, the SaaS Control Map forms the basis by which SaaS applications are evaluated, approved, implemented, monitored and terminated. Ultimately the SaaS Control Map defines the workflow by which SaaS applications are governed and managed with the specific activities recorded and documented.

When I initiate my conversation with clients on the importance of a SaaS Control Map, I find the discussion centers on SaaS-centric issues, missing the broader perspective necessary to establish the required comprehensive vision. I previously outlined the importance for SaaS Governance Enablers to form a multi-function, multi-discipline team. By doing so, SaaS Governance Enablers will have the opportunity to facilitate collaboration sessions in which team members will be able to contribute to development of a comprehensive workflow of an end-to-end series of requirements forming the basis of effective SaaS governance.

Each function we have targeted to participate in the SaaS Governance Team will have very different areas of focus and perspective on the issue. This multi-dimensional insight will be captured in the SaaS Control Map, enabling SaaS Governance Enablers and the SGT to build a detailed mapping of the policies, controls and requirements necessary to meet each life-cycle phase.

I have captured below some of the unique perspectives and insights I have encountered working with individuals from the following functional areas and disciplines. SaaS Governance Enablers need to take a moment to understand what will be important to each

Empowered SaaS Optimization - Tool 2
SaaS Control Map

SaaS Control Activity	Enterprise SaaS	Hybrid SaaS	HCM SaaS	Industry SaaS	*The Great Divide*	Functional SaaS	Task Specific SaaS	Service Specific SaaS	Misc. SaaS
Policy & Controls:									
Predefined Submission Process & Criteria	✓	✓	✓	✓		✓			
Rationalize Current Portfolio	✓	✓	✓	✓		✓	✓	✓	✓
Develop Requirements	✓	✓	✓	✓		✓	✓	✓	
SaaS Engagement/Use Policy & Consequence	✓	✓	✓	✓		✓	✓	✓	
Confirm need & funding: Purchase/Ongoing	✓	✓	✓	✓					
Evaluation & Approval:									
Internal Sign-off: InfoSec, Privacy, MDM	✓	✓	✓	✓		✓			
RFI - RFP Execution	✓	✓	✓	✓		✓			
Criteria development: InfoSec, TPRM, Privacy	✓	✓	✓	✓			✓		
Required Terms & Conditions	✓	✓	✓			✓	✓		
Contracting:									
Negotiation	✓	✓	✓	✓					
Basecase Confirmation	✓	✓	✓			✓			
Renewal Strategy/Planning				✓			✓		
SLA's & Transition Definition	✓	✓	✓			✓	✓	✓	
Go-Live / Implement:									
Education/Training support	✓	✓	✓	✓		✓			
Technical implementation support	✓	✓	✓			✓			
Incident resolution / ticket request	✓	✓	✓						
SaaS Management & Monitoring:									
Monitor & Measure Usage	✓	✓	✓	✓		✓	✓	✓	✓
Internal System alignment/integration	✓								
Demand Forecast	✓								
Renew / Cancel:									
Baseline consumption + Demand Forecast	✓	✓	✓	✓		✓	✓	✓	✓
Terms & Conditions Revision	✓	✓	✓	✓		✓			
Switch Scenario Model	✓	✓	✓	✓					

SaaS Control Map

participant in order to ensure they are comfortable contributing to the effort. Use the below as a guide to ensure the workshop is successful and you are able to accurately and completely develop the required SaaS requirements and controls.

- **Sourcing:** In many respects, Sourcing professionals have struggled to get their arms around the rapidly growing SaaS universe. Typically pulled into the discussion late in the process to achieve a 'save', Sourcing teams have limited ability to influence key terms and conditions as many times this has previously been agreed with the provider by the business unit or function owner.

  Sourcing professionals have the potential to be the key leader or SaaS Governance Enabler to establish SaaS policies and controls designed to limit unauthorized engagement of

SaaS without proper vetting and to determine the level of controls required over the course of the agreement.

Sourcing's focus for the SaaS Control Map will center around requirements to approve use of the SaaS application and activities to support renewal negotiations.

- **Vendor Management:** Technology Vendor Management (VMO) professionals are focused on service level management (SLAs) and monitoring that deliverables and obligations defined in the agreement are properly executed. The VMO also will take the lead with technology strategic vendor programs to support innovation and transformation efforts. This perspective is invaluable to SaaS Governance Enablers as they develop comprehensive monitoring and supplier engagement tactics to drive optimization on multiple levels.

- **Information Technology:** There is a prominent belief across IT that all SaaS is the responsibility of 'shadow IT' and IT is not required to support or be engaged in SaaS management. However, as Enterprise SaaS takes root and corporate developers configure and customize the SaaS platform, IT must be engaged to ensure business continuity and resilience is maintained. While IT's primary cloud focus has been in the areas of Infrastructure as a Service (IaaS) and Platform as a Service (PaaS), their engagement in development of SaaS policy, control and analysis of the proposed SaaS capabilities is critical to maintain operational alignment.

- **IT Finance:** They are typically surprised by unbudgeted SaaS spend. This can be both net new agreements that IT Finance was unaware of as well as mid-term true-up purchases. When it comes to optimization, IT Finance typically views claims of 'cost-avoidance' as fictitious. Preferring to book budget relief items they can document as 'hard save'. Having IT Finance as part of the SaaS Governance Team helps limit surprises, provides SaaS governance leaders insight to understand the best manner in which to report financial analysis to this very influential function who has the ear of the Chief Financial Officer and Chief Information Officer.

- **Software Asset Management:** As mentioned earlier, in many of my interviews with SaaS Management Platform executives, Software Asset Management (SAM) is not viewed as a key participant in SaaS governance and optimization efforts. It is the opinion and experience of *The Survival Guide to SaaS Optimization* that individuals assigned the responsibility to serve as administrators for SaaS portals have limited ability to produce the essential utilization analysis necessary to identify optimization opportunities. SAM professionals, with proper focus on license usage levels and license type optimization data can triangulate analysis with other internal information sources. SAM professionals can bring real value to the SaaS Governance Team with detailed analysis, trending and ongoing harvest of user licenses, identify unused platform assets and support identification of potential non-compliance in hybrid SaaS segment partners. In addition, with the strong growth of Enterprise and Hybrid SaaS segment offerings that have a potential component of license compliance requirements, SAM professionals will bring that valuable experience to the team.

- **Information Security:** A very important group to include in the SaaS Governance Team is Information Security (InfoSec). As SaaS partners become a greater concentration of the technology environment, establishing and maintaining diligence of potential vulnerabilities is essential. InfoSec needs to be core contributors to requirements for SaaS partners in these important areas across the entire SaaS life cycle. In addition, InfoSec will be able to define minimal acceptable security requirements for SaaS partners and potential audit and due diligence approaches to confirm compliance.

- **TPRM/GRC:** A more prevalent function in regulated industries, Third Party Risk Management (TRPM) and Governance, Risk & Compliance (GRC) bring to the SaaS Governance Team a focus on developing evidence and activities necessary to monitor SaaS partners in order to identify emerging risk that could lead to operational disruption. Increasingly, SaaS services represent a growing percent of a company's third parties and an area of focus for regulators. Having representation in the SGT from this function will help strengthen development of policies and controls for SaaS evaluation and selection. Additionally, in collaboration with Vendor Management, Risk professionals will have excellent insight to activities to monitor and perform due diligence activities when required.

The Survival Guide to SaaS Optimization believes compliance and risk management will continue to grow in importance for organizations as they attempt to establish effective SaaS governance practices. Compliance leaders will become a powerful influence and ally to establish comprehensive SaaS governance and optimization practices in all regulated entities.

The above list of functions for participation in the SaaS Governance Team has been provided as a suggestion for SaaS Governance Enablers to bring SaaS governance and optimization to the forefront of their organization. Additional teams that can be considered include Privacy and Internal Audit (IA) as they will also have concerns with SaaS governance practices and establishing the proper policies and controls by which SaaS partners are evaluated, monitored with appropriate documentation to serve as evidence to satisfy regulatory requirements.

Now that we have discussed the individual perspectives of various professionals targeted to participate as member of the SaaS Governance Team, the goal for SaaS Governance Enablers is to orchestrate these perspectives to develop a comprehensive series of policies, controls and measures across the full SaaS partner life cycle workflow. Having detailed controls for evaluation, selection and onboarding with little to no ongoing monitoring or analysis misses the emergence of risk and lost optimization. Conversely, allowing any SaaS partner to be engaged with limited upfront controls but detailed usage analysis ignores risk and potential regulatory compliance challenges. Our team of assembled professionals will ensure appropriate policy and control activities across the end-to-end SaaS partner life cycle.

SaaS Control Map Phases

The Survival Guide to SaaS Optimization has defined a 6-phase SaaS Control Map structure. In each individual phase, the goal for SaaS Governance Enablers and members of the SaaS Governance Team is to strike a balance that produces the required detail to establish and maintain effective policies and controls versus creating unnecessary bureaucratic overhead. The multi-function, multi-discipline composition of the SaaS Governance Team will ensure each phase of the SaaS Control Map has appropriate requirements and sub-task that support organization-wide SaaS governance requirements and a clear, easy to follow workflow for the business to follow.

- **Policy & Controls:** Perhaps this is obvious, but many organizations have yet to establish dedicated, specific policies and controls related to the use of SaaS services. Many simply amend or edit existing policies for software or IT use, but this falls short in addressing the uniqueness of SaaS services. An additional dynamic evident across the SaaS community is the emergence of a 'tool-first' approach to discovering SaaS in the corporate environment. *The Survival Guide to SaaS Optimization* believes this to be a serious error if the initial focused activity ignores development of appropriate SaaS policies and controls and the accountability of employees to adhere to these stated policies. When effectively communicated and enforced with clear accountability and consequence, the simple action of creating SaaS policies and controls enables organizations to understand their SaaS universe and identify non-compliant SaaS usage.

Policy: The ESO framework recommends development of a dedicated SaaS Policy that defines the requirement to go through the approval workflow defined by the SaaS Governance Team. The SaaS Policy should be clear on:

o Approval Process

o Criteria by which approval will be granted

o Accountability of the individual to engage the SaaS Governance Team and utilize the established approval workflow

o Consequence for non-compliance

o Purchase guidelines and requirements

Control: The central theme and focus of SaaS Controls is how to monitor and maintain an accurate and complete list of SaaS providers in the environment and quickly identify areas of non-compliance. Controls will be closely aligned and coordinated with Information Security, Third Party Risk Management, Governance, Risk & Compliance as well as purchasing and procurement.

- **Evaluation & Approval:** With clearly defined SaaS Policy and Controls, the SaaS Control Map moves to the next phase or stage of the SaaS life cycle which is structured to address the criteria by which SaaS capabilities will be evaluated and approved for inclusion in the corporate environment. Utilizing the diverse perspective of the SaaS Governance Team, SaaS Governance Enablers should develop the appropriate requirements by SaaS segment. *The Survival Guide to SaaS Optimization* has observed that it is the functional, tactical and miscellaneous SaaS services that receive the quickest approval and least due diligence yet can represent the most significant risk and optimization challenges. The goal will be to have many of the evaluation and approval criteria automated and easy to document for these segments to achieve the desired balance of diligence and path to implementation.

- **Contracting:** To date, contracting of SaaS services has been highly distributed across an organization producing a wide-array of terms and conditions that may not be advantageous to the organization. Much of this is due to the independent activity of business units or functions determined to access tools that will support their business goals and objectives. This ultimately puts Sourcing at a disadvantage as the SaaS provider has essentially received approval from the budget owners and Sourcing is tasked with saving some funds.

  In addition to achieving a level of consistency for terms and conditions across SaaS segments, centralization of SaaS negotiations and determination of set language for SaaS agreements reduces operational and regulatory risk. Items of importance include service levels, termination, data ownership, data access, data storage and several other items.

  The final key criteria for contracting will be review and approval by the SaaS Governance Team and sign-off by Sourcing with the executive sponsor of the SaaS service identified and informed of their accountability to adhere to SaaS governance and optimization requirements.

- **Go Live / Implement:** SaaS may not initially require a great deal of technical support, however when issues do arise, teams using the SaaS capability need to understand where to go for resolution. This is best achieved by education and effective communications to the universe of users. During this phase it is important Vendor Management can effectively onboard the SaaS partner and take control of the deliverables and obligations (D&O) defined in the agreement and by which performance will be assessed.

The Survival Guide to SaaS Optimization recommends the SGT establishes a set process by SaaS segment including utilization of a Proof of Concept (POC), establishing a group of 'power-users' combined with a team to have SaaS platform initiation review meetings to help develop deep user knowledge in order to maximize benefits realized. All activities are intended to help the SGT ensure teams are able to fully utilize the SaaS capability while also gaining insight to platform usage which will help the VMO team when reporting license type and license usage from the tenant.

- **Management & Monitoring:** This is the area of the SaaS life cycle that currently represents the most significant challenge for organizations. Much has been written about the level of wasted spend with Gartner, Zylo and others estimating levels to be at 30% of total SaaS investment. Based on Gartner's forecast of the global SaaS market to reach $104.7 Billion as 2020 comes to a close, that means organizations have the opportunity to reclaim over $30 Billion in SaaS spend on an annual basis. *The Survival Guide to SaaS Optimization* and the Empowered SaaS Optimization Framework has been developed to help organizations develop the strategies and tactics to address this important opportunity.

  However, for SaaS Governance Enablers to understand true optimization is far more than simple usage management. This is why it is so important for the SaaS Governance Team to include Vendor Management, Third Party Risk Management, Governance, Risk & Compliance and Information Security as SaaS Management Life Cycle activities must include effective monitoring and ongoing risk assessment activities. Development of the SaaS Control Map, ESO framework Tool 2, supports grounding the multi-discipline team and guiding them to develop the appropriate monitoring, assessment and due diligence activities that compliment license and usage management.

It is the opinion of *The Survival Guide to SaaS Optimization* that in addition to Sourcing executives, as Compliance and Information Security executives increase focus on the risk and vulnerabilities unmanaged SaaS portfolio presents to an organization, the decision to establish a dedicated SaaS governance and optimization function will grow.

- **Renew/Cancel:** Currently, SaaS governance activities have primarily been around contract renewals. Typically, Sourcing is brought into the discussion very late in the process and are only able to affect the final outcome to a small degree, leading to a less than desired outcome. The goal of establishing a dedicated SaaS focus in the form of a multi-discipline team, is to formalize structured end to end criteria and elements necessary to achieve effective governance across all phases of the life cycle. The culmination of these activities, outlined in the ESO framework SaaS Control Map, is the ability to negotiate SaaS agreements and renewals aligned to actual usage while ensuring the services are aligned with defined requirements including security, privacy and risk areas.

SaaS providers can have any number of potential renewal strategies including the traditional 3-year renewal cycles of Independent Software Vendors (ISV) all the way to monthly renewals. Tool 1 of the ESO framework, SaaS Active User Roster, forms the basis for developing a SaaS renewal calendar to support prioritization of renewal activities and development of the required information to drive optimization and efficiency.

A last key item to ensure is included in the SaaS Renew or Cancel portion of the SaaS Control Map are activities to cover the potential of transitioning from one SaaS provider to another or elimination of the service and transitioning to internal IT support. SaaS providers continually attempt to increase their leverage by making the ability to switch to another service nearly impossible. SaaS Governance Enablers need to carefully monitor this dynamic and work with the internal SaaS executive sponsor to ensure flexibility is maintained and negotiation leverage is not compromised.

While *The Survival Guide to SaaS Optimization* utilizes a 6-phase SaaS Control Map, it is important to understand the level of diligence, monitoring and required controls should vary by SaaS segment. While each stage will have several sub-tasks, not all will be required or relevant for each SaaS provider based on their previously identified and assigned segment. This enables SaaS Governance Enablers to apply the appropriate level of governance to achieve the desired optimization of the SaaS universe for each individual SaaS capability. Refinement of the SaaS Control Map workflows based on SaaS application segment also supports the business need for quick and effective implementation of SaaS capabilities.

SaaS Control Map Segment Alignment

The goal of Tool 2 of the ESO framework, 'SaaS Control Map', is to provide a visible guide of potential criteria that can be applied to the evaluation of a SaaS capability based upon the assigned SaaS segment. With control criteria developed by a cross-functional team of operational experts, the SaaS Governance Team has considered a broad range of issues to create a comprehensive, end to end approach to determining suitability and sustainability of a SaaS partner.

The visual of the SaaS Control Map provided here is intended to serve as an example. Working collaboratively, the SaaS Governance Team should define appropriate SaaS requirements for your organization and create sub-task for each lifecycle phase to achieve the desired detail. Aligning sub-task requirement by SaaS segment quickly informs internal SaaS sponsors the expectation and effort that will be required to safely secure approval of their selected SaaS application and capability.

For those of you from a risk or compliance discipline, you will quickly see the value a SaaS Control Map provides when dealing with Internal Audit or external regulators. It forms a powerful visual as well as an effective guide for these professionals to validate and confirm compliance or identify areas of potential deficiency with recommended improvements.

As mentioned earlier, the goal is not to create an overwhelming bureaucratic process but a logical, well-structured and straight forward workflow that clearly demonstrates an effective balance between managing risk and enabling the organization to quickly engage a SaaS capability to achieve their desired outcome.

The SaaS Control Map example provided is intended to show the number of items required to receive approval to proceed with a specific SaaS partner and the following measures by which the SaaS capability will be assessed to ensure proper governance and optimization is maintained. These requirements should be aligned by the specific defined segment for the service in question. There should be significant difference between the requirement for an Enterprise SaaS application selection versus a tactical, individual function or business unit SaaS tool. It is easy to overwhelm your organization when these new policies, controls and procedures are designed and ultimately implemented. The SaaS Governance Team should continually ask is this a 'must have' or a 'nice to have'.

Based on my experience supporting multiple clients in developing their specific SaaS Control Map, *The Survival Guide to SaaS Optimization* provides the following insight to help SaaS Governance Enablers develop the key task for each SaaS segment.

- **Enterprise SaaS Control Map Considerations:** This category of SaaS provider typically will see the full range of activities defined in the SaaS Control Map; however, they may be executed differently than the remaining SaaS segments.

Many times, Enterprise SaaS selection will utilize a formal RFP process controlled by sourcing and supported by several functional areas based on the specific capability being considered. Due to the size of investment, there is high probability there will be a series of financial gates for final approval.

The challenge that has historically impacted the Enterprise SaaS segment has been the uncoordinated engagement of business unit leaders and budget owners who independently work with a SaaS provider such as Salesforce to secure capabilities they believe necessary to deliver their business plan. The most effective means to address this is clearly defined SaaS policies and controls with defined accountability and consequence for independent, non-compliant engagement. When combined with proactive vendor management efforts, organizations can achieve highly coordinated activities across the shadow-IT landscape. Establishing the desired leverage to achieve greater overall results for the organization and business unit leaders.

- **Hybrid SaaS Control Map Considerations:** This category will represent a significant challenge for the foreseeable future as traditional perpetual on-premise licenses convert to subscription models. Many ISV's are doing module by module conversions as they introduce the next version of their product. Coordination across an organization's traditional IT sourcing, IT vendor management and SaaS Governance Team is needed to ensure proper assessment of the new subscription services against the criteria set forth in the ESO framework's SaaS Control Map.

Information Security and Third Party Risk Management will be very interested in these activities to ensure appropriate business continuity measures are maintained and vulnerabilities are identified and managed. In addition, Software Asset Management will be able to provide guidance and insight on potential issues related to software compliance.

- **Human Capital Management SaaS Control Map Considerations:** Due to the separated nature of Human Capital Management (HCM) SaaS platforms, it is important to ensure alignment with Information Security and other functional areas to identify process gaps that could lead to unnecessary vulnerabilities. While SuccessFactors and Workday dominate this category, there are many new entrants in this space that will require close evaluation and assessment to determine their capabilities meet or exceed requirements defined in the SaaS Control Map.

- **Industry SaaS Control Map Considerations:** In many respects, SaaS capabilities in this segment are in fact the core ERP solutions on which these businesses depend. As such, they receive similar diligence to the Enterprise SaaS segment described above. A caveat may be these SaaS providers could be more susceptible to a change in ownership and merger and acquisition activity. To address this, utilizing core vendor management principles and applying quality and applying quality Third Party Risk Management (TPRM) and Governance, Risk and Compliance (GRC) measures should prove sufficient.

- **Functional, Task & Service Specific, Miscellaneous SaaS Control Map Considerations:** These segments have been combined as the characteristics are very similar, however it is important to keep them separate for reporting, analysis and identification. To date, the focus of SaaS governance and optimization in these categories has been license usage, however the lack of clear SaaS policies and controls has led to potential regularity risk due to the information and data that may reside in these non-compliant locations. In addition to unidentified, unmonitored potential risk, *The Survival Guide to SaaS Optimization* continually observes significant levels of redundant SaaS capabilities as most organizations are yet to coordinate or consolidate SaaS portfolios in a SaaS catalogue.

As SaaS Governance Enablers and SaaS Governance Team members build out elements of the SaaS Control Map and corresponding workflow, the following dynamics must be considered for each of these SaaS segments.

- Due to the volume, it is critical to establish clear Polices to address the selection, implementation and payment of SaaS services.

- Polices need to carry very real consequence for non-compliance

- Centralization and approved procurement paths are necessary to maintain a level of accuracy and establish appropriate Controls.

- Controls should include appropriate business unit or functional approval process to ensure accountability.

- An executive sponsor must be assigned with acknowledgment of the assignment recorded. This individual must be at a senior level in the organization.

- Document Executive owner's business unit and cost center

- Due to volume, renewal management processes must be streamlined to ensure license type and usage optimization is produced in sufficient time to support negotiations.

- Ability to extract the required usage data is clearly assigned with scheduled reporting and analysis.

The goal of these measures is to ensure alignment of SaaS governance activities that address all internal function and discipline requirements while supporting business requirements.

Summary: ESO Tool 1 & Tool 2

Before we proceed, I want to take a moment to summarize what I believe to be the key actions we as SaaS Governance Enablers have accomplished to this point in the Empowered SaaS Optimization framework.

As SaaS Governance Enablers, we have:

- Facilitated the formation of a multi-function, multi-discipline team to function as a SaaS Governance Team

- We have developed a segmentation strategy by which each SaaS capability and application will be assigned

- Utilizing the SaaS Active Universe Roster (ESO Tool 1), we have created a central, comprehensive summary of our organizations SaaS portfolio.

- With the SaaS portfolio defined, we next gathered the collective expertise of our SaaS Governance Team to create a comprehensive, multi-phase SaaS Control Map (ESO Tool 2) to establish the core criteria by which SaaS partners are evaluated, engaged, monitored and removed. Producing a balanced governance platform on which optimization, risk mitigation and security vulnerabilities will be monitored.

The Survival Guide to SaaS Optimization now turns attention to defining the detailed governance framework necessary to establish the foundation for effective, ongoing SaaS governance and optimization. The third tool of the Empowered SaaS Optimization framework is the SaaS Governance Framework.

SaaS Governance Framework

ESO Tool 3, the SaaS Governance Framework, is designed to identify the core activities of a SaaS application life cycle and define the corresponding roles and responsibilities of key functional areas for each of the specified activities. Structured like a RACI (Responsible – Accountable – Consult – Inform), the SaaS Governance Framework provides an easy visual for SaaS Governance Enablers to collaborate with SGT members.

A word of warning for SaaS Governance Enablers. When I work with clients to facilitate the SaaS Control Map workshop, I find participants are very engaged providing excellent input to the steps and actions they want to have included in each of the SaaS Control Map phases. As I turn the conversation to development of the SaaS Governance Framework, these same individuals will sit back in their chairs and go silent or dismiss the activity as just another RACI. My message to the team is that development of the SaaS Governance Framework is to ensure they are only pulled into relevant issues and their contribution to SaaS governance and optimization is then more focused and surgical than a large, non-productive time commitment.

Tool 3, SaaS Governance Framework, focuses on defining the components of an effective SaaS governance framework and defining the roles and responsibilities of those key individuals who will help define and manage a broad, coordinated SaaS management capability. The purpose of which is to know who is on point for each phase, when and where handoffs occur within the identified areas and ultimate accountability to deliver the SaaS governance agenda. SaaS Governance Enablers need to remain focused on this goal and objective and keep the team focused and on point or run the risk of having the SaaS Governance Framework become an overbearing structure. Try not to exceed 7 core activities of a SaaS governance and optimization life cycle but push the team to define at least 5 at the minimum.

SaaS Governance Framework: Core Activities

Based on my experience and those of the SaaS leaders I work with and interviewed, *The Survival Guide to SaaS Optimization* defines a SaaS Governance Framework that features 7 distinct and separate core activities. Each of these core activities has multiple sub-tasks, however the sub-task will be highly customized based upon the unique dynamics of your organization. I have found that as SaaS discussions occur with multiple disciplines in an organization, a SaaS-centric definition of a governance framework is quickly expanded to view the broader implications of SaaS applications in the corporate environment. I have found the typical 4 phase SaaS life cycle promoted by so many of the SaaS Management Platforms and advisory firms of 'discover, optimize, plan and govern' approach lacks an understanding of the depth and requirements of functional teams such as Compliance, Risk, Privacy and Information Security leaders. With insight to the needs of these critical disciplines, the ESO framework engages these individuals as part of the SaaS Governance Team, secures their input into the SaaS Control Map and ensures their predefined roles and responsibilities over the defined core activities of the SaaS Governance Framework.

The Survival Guide to SaaS Optimization has defined 7 individual core activities for the SaaS Governance Framework. Each of these core activities has a series of task that need to be accomplished with clear 'Go/No-Go' criteria and hand-off requirements.

1. **Executive Sponsorship Strategy:** Enlisting the sponsorship of a highly visible and influential executive sponsor is key for the SaaS Governance Enabler to achieve success. To date, many organizations have turned to the Chief Information Officer (CIO) to play this role. While it is easy to view this as an appropriate approach, there is an increased risk this will not be effective as any attempt by CIO's to grab hold of business-oriented SaaS capabilities may be met with political resistance from the business executives. Many of

Empowered SaaS Optimization - Tool 3
SaaS Governance Framework

R = Responsible
A = Accountable
C = Consulted
I = Inform

Roles & Responsibilities

SaaS Governance Framework — Core Activities	IT Exec		BU Exec		Sourcing		VMO		Compliance		InfoSec		Privacy		IA		SAM	
	E,H,I Group	F,T,M Group	E,H,I Group	F,T,M Group	E,H,I Group	F,T,M Group	E,H,I Group	F,T,M Group	E,H,I Group	F,T,M Group	E,H,I Group	F,T,M Group	E,H,I Group	F,T,M Group	E,H,I Group	F,T,M Group	E,H,I Group	F,T,M Group
Executive Sponsor Strategy																		
Roadmap Development & Strategy																		
Rules of Engagement																		
Monitor & Assess																		
Measure & Analysis																		
Usage Baseline Management																		
Renewal Management																		

SaaS Governance Framework

whom see their use of shadow IT and SaaS to support their specific needs as a budget right.

The Survival Guide to SaaS Optimization has found SaaS Governance Enablers and their organizations are most successful when the executive sponsor is the Chief Financial Officer (CFO), a direct report to the CFO such as the head of Sourcing or the executive responsible for Compliance, typically the Chief Compliance Officer or Risk Officer. To secure the engagement of these executives, SaaS Governance Enablers should leverage the output defined in the Active SaaS Universe Roster (ESO Tool 1) to quantify the extent of SaaS in the corporate environment, distribution of this SaaS usage across the various business units and a rough forecast of anticipated SaaS growth. Combining this information with publicly available statements from leading consulting organizations such as Gartner who estimate 30% of SaaS spend is wasted should help grab the CFO's attention and commitment to be the executive sponsor.

Chief Compliance or Risk Officers will also be very interested in the Active SaaS Universe Roster (ESO Tool 1). However, when the SaaS Governance Enablers is able to combine this information with the output from an initial SaaS Control Map (ESO Tool 2), these executives react positively to the focus on policies, controls, pre-engagement requirements and ongoing monitoring.

I do want to stress a point though before we leave the importance of securing effective and visible executive sponsorship. I have had the opportunity to help multiple organizations design and implement SaaS management programs. In every case, when the SaaS governance message focuses on SaaS application redundancy, subscription centralization and license utilization, the executives targeted to be the sponsor for SaaS governance politely direct the conversation continue with one of their operational or department manager. Conversely, when the SaaS governance message presented to these executives offers a balanced focus of optimization with regulatory compliance, security vulnerability identification and risk management, these same executives have stepped-up to assume executive sponsorship.

Go/No-Go: Consideration of a new SaaS application or capability must have the appropriate executive sponsor and identified cost center for budget tracking. If there is no executive sponsor for the SaaS application meeting the required criteria, the application will not be endorsed.

2. **Roadmap Development & Strategy:** With executive sponsorship secured, the next critical component of the SaaS Governance Framework is to hold sessions with your organizations business unit leaders and technology leaders. The goal for SaaS Governance Enablers is to align business priorities with expected digital transformation services necessary to deliver the required innovation. Many of the technology enablers discussed during these meetings will be Enterprise, Hybrid or Industry SaaS services, but others will be from categories specific to business unit need or function with IT having limited knowledge or involvement. Many times, this is the area referred to as 'shadow-IT', but in my opinion shadow-IT is a legacy term that sets-up a natural conflict between business units and IT. I prefer to look at the use of cloud-based SaaS applications and services as a means to accelerate a capability to benefit business outcome and refer to these as 'business enablers'. The goal of the SaaS Governance Enablers is to make certain these services adhere to the stated policies and controls, undergo the required onboarding process and vetting, and are included in ongoing governance and monitoring requirements, ultimately ensuring business units receive optimal value of their business enablers with risk and vulnerabilities continually monitored.

Go/No-Go: Confirm the SaaS application being considered is a technology or business enabler that aligns with the business unit's strategy versus a tactical tool for no apparent strategic purpose.

3. **Rules of Engagement:** Efforts to establish an effective SaaS governance framework quickly breakdown when roles and responsibilities for interaction with SaaS providers is left undefined. Due to the nature of SaaS services, account managers for various SaaS providers gain easy entry to an organization, exploiting the natural interest of individual functions or disciplines across an enterprise. Separately, there are a significant number of SaaS applications that can be engaged by signing-up online with a credit card. This is an area where discovery capability of a dedicated SaaS Management Platform can be of value to augment the implementation of SaaS policies and controls.

   As we have seen with the number of SaaS segments, no 'one size fits all' exist when it comes to establishing Rules of Engagement for SaaS capabilities. Shortly we will discuss the importance of developing Rules of Engagement (RoE) by SaaS segment. This will enable the individual business unit teams to have the appropriate interactions to maintain independence but hold these interactions in a coordinated, predefined manner to ensure alignment with organization requirements defined in the SaaS Control Map (ESO Tool 2).

   Core to the concept for Rules of Engagement is defined consequence for non-compliance in the form of a detailed comprehensive SaaS policy with clear boundaries. This is where a SaaS platform and close monitoring of software purchases both in approved and non-approved procurement channels such as P-Cards, will enable the SaaS Governance Enablers to identify and report non-compliance. Due to the severe consequence an organization will face if they inadvertently compromise regulations such as Europe's

General Data Protection Regulation (GDPR) or Personally Identifiable Information (PII), compliance leadership will actively support RoE requirements as will Information Security who are focused on vulnerability management.

Vendor Management, Sourcing and Third Party Risk Management professionals are very familiar with the concept of Rules of Engagement and should be able to help guide the SaaS Governance Team to develop an excellent structure. Take the time to develop appropriate Rules of Engagement for the identified logical groupings who may interface with SaaS provider account teams including business unit leaders, functional leaders, operational teams, technology teams.

Go/No-Go: Clearly defined Rules of Engagement for business and technology owners with documented acceptance and accountability for non-compliance.

4. **Monitor & Assess:** There is a natural separation of monitoring requirements based on SaaS segment. SaaS partners providing Enterprise, Hybrid and Industry SaaS capabilities will be monitored through a combination of vendor management practices in addition to SaaS specific license consumption and platform usage. Third Party Risk Management will apply additional monitoring tactics to assess SaaS partner viability and sustainability. Fortunately, the number of SaaS providers in this category will be a manageable subset of the SaaS universe.

   As we shift focus from Enterprise, Hybrid and Industry SaaS segment groupings, monitoring approach and tactics change significantly. As this is the largest portion of an organizations SaaS population and is typically dispersed throughout operations, automation is required to maintain a reasonable level of monitoring to identify and mitigate emerging risk before disruption or loss occurs. SaaS Governance Teams will again benefit from inclusion of Third

Party Risk Management, Governance Risk and Compliance and InfoSec participation as they bring an insight of the best tactics to monitor a SaaS partners viability. The level of data access and type of data populated in the SaaS application will be a major determinant of how extensive and frequent audit and due diligence efforts may be required of a SaaS capability. Smaller SaaS providers present an organization a disproportionate level of risk due to probability of failure or acquisition, leading to potential operational disruption.

In addition to a SaaS Management Platform, with the input of TPRM and GRC team members, SaaS Governance Enablers need to consider news feeds and social media outlets that will trigger notifications pertaining to any changes for these SaaS providers in order to extend overall monitoring efforts.

Go/No-Go: SaaS Management Platform has been implemented combined with additional reporting from SaaS application portals has been aligned with targeted report extracts to populate a predefined monitoring and assessment requirement of prioritized SaaS applications.

5. **Measure & Analysis:** Before we can manage SaaS usage to targeted levels, we need to establish the tactics necessary to generate the required ongoing measurement and analysis to drive the desired outcome. In the current world of SaaS, organizations have been lulled into a false sense of security with aggregate level usage data being viewed as the basis for determining SaaS optimization. The unfortunate reality is few organizations today have applied the necessary focus to determine the depth of what can be extracted from the SaaS application tenant or portal, relying instead on usage reporting provided by the SaaS account team.

Aligned by segment, the SaaS Governance Team needs to define the level or depth of reporting necessary to achieve and maintain optimal license type management and usage. As stated earlier, I find the largest universe of a clients SaaS applications will be in the functional, tactical or miscellaneous segments. Regardless if your firm has a SaaS management platform, a common level of usage reporting for the designated SaaS segment needs to be extracted from the various portals on a scheduled basis for executive sponsors and stakeholders. If you do have a SaaS Management Platform, utilize the reporting to form the foundation and enhance the analysis with the additional usage data downloaded from the SaaS partner tenant.

Go/No-Go: Designated point of contact who will be provided data on a scheduled basis and the source of the 'upstream' data to be provided at the designated time.

6. **Usage Baseline Management:** Building upon the analysis produced in the 5th component of the SaaS Governance Framework, SaaS Governance Enablers now have the data necessary to forecast and trend SaaS usage across the SaaS partner and application landscape. Maintaining optimal usage baseline measurement requires careful identification of other internal data sources to perform data triangulation, extending the web of data points for license type and license usage analysis while identifying potential process improvement opportunities.

    As mentioned in the Measure and Analysis portion of the SaaS Governance Framework, current focus of SaaS Governance Enablers is on aggregate license usage reporting. Applying the internal discipline to dig deeper into all available portal usage data for SaaS applications and comparing license consumption with internal data sources such as Active Directory, will help SaaS Governance Enablers gain a broader and deeper understanding of SaaS baseline usage.

Go/No-Go: Assignment of the individuals who will receive the analysis and action recommendations

7. **Renewal Management:** *The Survival Guide to SaaS Optimization* has aligned the SaaS life cycle to seven distinct components, ending with SaaS Renewal Management. To establish quality governance practices and achieve an optimized SaaS portfolio, detail must be paid to the numerous activities required to enable effective renewal management. This is far more than simply knowing when the renewal is due and attempting to plan ahead. The Active SaaS Universe Roster (Tool 1), the initial tool and recommended activity of the Empowered SaaS Optimization (ESO) framework supports identification of renewal date, frequency of renewal and potential clauses that can influence the actions necessary to prepare and develop an internal SaaS renewal calendar.

   The Active SaaS Universe Roster (ESO Tool 1) also identifies the executive sponsor for the specific SaaS application renewal. This helps SaaS Governance Enablers and Sourcing leaders ensure awareness of who is to be on point to ensure quick, direct access to the key decision maker and likely budget holder. It is recommended SaaS Governance Enablers support internal preliminary conversations with the identified executive sponsor supported by current usage analysis, baseline management measures and current forecast. Again, the focus is for the activities of the SaaS Governance Team to add value and help SaaS executive sponsors receive maximum value from their specific SaaS application investment while continually monitoring risk and potential security vulnerabilities.

   Renewal management activities include:

   o   Identification of key team including authorizer

- o Key terms and conditions to be revised to reflect current realities

- o Addition of net new terms such as future price increase caps or limits

- o Review of internal demand and requirements across the SaaS user base and executive sponsor

- o Review potential merger and acquisition activities that could impact usage and license requirements

- o Clarity on negotiation roles and responsibilities

Go/No-Go: Define timing by which SaaS usage analysis is to be provided to Sourcing to support renewal optimization efforts.

The Survival Guide to SaaS Optimization now builds upon the 7 Core Activities of ESO Tool 3 SaaS Governance Framework to explore the roles and responsibilities of those individuals who contribute to required governance and optimization activities.

SaaS Governance Framework: Roles & Responsibilities

As a SaaS engagement moves across the defined core activities, the involvement of participants in SaaS governance will also shift as will the roles and responsibilities. The critical element for SaaS Governance Enablers is to ensure linkage, alignment and strong coordination across all identified parties to facilitate rapid resolution of open items. This places emphasis on active and frequent communications supported by analysis to ensure all engaged in SaaS governance and optimization remain informed.

SaaS governance is most effective when roles and responsibilities are clearly defined, and specific actions or required decisions are aligned to an individual's functional expertise. While this may shift from organization to organization, I have consistently observed the following dynamics emerge when SaaS issues are debated by

SaaS Governance Enablers, executive sponsors and operational stakeholders.

- **IT Executive:** Having IT executive sponsorship and support for definition of a SaaS Governance Framework will help ensure any SaaS issues related to roadmap alignment and Rules of Engagement (RoE) can be addressed effectively.

- **Business Unit Executive:** Ensuring these business leaders are aware and have actively provided input to the measures by which SaaS services are assessed, governed and optimized is an important element to establishing alignment and gaining their support.

- **Sourcing:** To be clear, Sourcing is the key orchestrator of SaaS governance and optimization activities across all 7 Core Activities of the SaaS Governance Framework. They either lead the activity or are highly involved with ensuring the task is successfully executed.

- **Vendor Management:** Closely aligned with Sourcing, Vendor Management representation forms an important bond across the majority of SaaS lifecycle governance activities. While Vendor Management will be primarily involved with governance activities for enterprise, hybrid and industry SaaS segments, they will be an important input to the automation strategies for governing the remaining segments.

- **Software Asset Management:** Software Asset Management (SAM) representation in the SaaS Governance Team and participation across the SaaS lifecycle supports more analytical view of usage data to enable greater optimization. Driving beyond simple aggregate usage reporting to deliver real savings and cost avoidance.

- **IT Finance:** While IT Finance may be a passive function across SaaS Governance Framework phases, they receive tremendous value by being aware of all reporting, analysis and activity of the SaaS Governance Team.

- **Information Security (InfoSec):** Another team that will benefit from active participation in development and maintenance of the Active SaaS Universe Roster (ESO Tool 1) and ongoing tracking that new SaaS partners in the environment is Information Security. They are a key input to the SaaS Control Map (Tool 2 of the ESO framework) and are a valued input throughout each core activity of the SaaS Governance framework.

- **Third Party Risk Management / Governance, Risk & Compliance:** The requirement to categorize third parties, determine monitoring criteria to assess emerging risk and developing pre-determined steps necessary to remove a third party without operational impact is an important perspective for the SaaS Governance Team. Professionals from this discipline are invaluable to reinforcing SaaS governance and optimization is much more than a renewal discount achieved.

- **Privacy:** With a recent rash of rulings with significant judgments from European Regulators concerning mismanagement of customer information, if your organization has a Privacy function, they would be an excellent addition to the SaaS Governance Team with input to the SaaS Control Map (ESO Tool 2) and ensure sensitivity to privacy requirements throughout SaaS Governance Framework phases.

- **Internal Audit:** If your organization has an Internal Audit (IA) function, their involvement with development of SaaS governance policies and controls defined in the SaaS Control Map will produce positive results when an audit is executed.

SaaS Governance Framework: Segment Grouping

I have covered the Core Activities of the SaaS Governance Framework (ESO Tool 3) and the cross-functional teams' roles and responsibilities to successfully perform these core activities. It's now time to overlay the SaaS segment structure developed as part of the SaaS Active Universe Roster (ESO Tool 1) with the SaaS Governance Framework (ESO Tool 3) to ensure an appropriate level of diligence is applied based on the SaaS partner's assigned segment and the anticipated volume of SaaS applications in the specific segment. *The Survival Guide to SaaS Optimization* recommends SaaS Governance Enablers establish two separate SaaS Governance Framework RACI's to ensure the SaaS Governance Team does not become overwhelmed or apply unnecessary workflow requirements.

- **E-H-I Group RACI Dynamics:** Enterprise, Hybrid and true Industry SaaS services will naturally have a higher degree of visibility across corporate and IT executives as these are the services that support core business operations. Engagement of these senior positions will require detailed analysis and technology roadmap alignment to business services. There should be heightened focus and careful review of SaaS partner viability as operational disruption could occur if the application is core to operations. For this reason, *The Survival Guide to SaaS Optimization* recommends the SaaS Governance Team take the time to create a dedicated SaaS Governance RACI for providers in these identified categories. It is also important to include the Human Capital Management SaaS platform as well to this RACI structure.

- **F-T-M Group RACI Dynamics:** Governance of SaaS partners in the remaining categories of Functional, Tactical or Miscellaneous categories will have less importance to executives but will be of great interest to business or functional sponsors of the SaaS application. Due to the volume of SaaS providers in these categories, reporting and analysis become the priority. The RACI must support rapid decision making based upon standardized criteria, continually updated usage information and current risk measures.

The Survival Guide to SaaS Optimization recommends development of the SaaS Governance Framework (RACI) is done so in a focused workshop with the core members of the SaaS Governance Team. Once completed, the team should use the opportunity to present the final output to the SaaS executive sponsors and stakeholders. The goal being to have these individuals understand the strategic value of the RACI and its alignment with the other core SaaS governance templates including the Active SaaS Universe Roster and the SaaS Control Map.

SaaS Governance Misnomer

Before we leave Part 1 SaaS Governance, there is a final important item to be discussed as I have found in my dealings with clients there is a dangerous misconception that continually exposes organizations to inefficient management of their SaaS portfolio. This misconception centers in one of two areas: the role of Shadow IT and the scope of a Cloud Center of Excellence (CCOE). The unfortunate by-product of these misconceptions is little to no active governance or optimization of an organizations SaaS portfolio creating unnecessary exposure, risk and waste.

- **Shadow IT:** Shadow IT has been Information Technologies nemesis for decades. The threat of business owners pulling funding to support corporate initiatives and take matters into their own hands is not new. The rapid growth and pervasive nature of SaaS applications in organizations today has been consistently blamed on shadow IT across the business. But what is shadow IT and are they really trying to steal the thunder of a central IT organization?

  Business leaders and their operational teams are continually under pressure to achieve 'plan'. SaaS applications offer compelling capabilities that can be implemented rapidly to support execution of this targeted, business unit agenda. As discussed earlier, much of the SaaS usage employed by business units fits the SaaS categories of Functional, Tactical or miscellaneous segments, representing the largest volume of SaaS partners in the corporate environment. However, business unit associates referred to as Shadow IT have limited appetite to support governance of the SaaS services they have enabled as their sole focus is on plan achievement.

Rarely do the business units that have engaged a SaaS application to support their operation take the necessary actions to optimize and maintain license counts, preferring to simply increase levels when informed they need to do so by the provider. Many times, these individuals we have labeled 'shadow IT' have no idea how to access the SaaS portal to generate user level usage analysis, preferring to have the SaaS provider submit aggregate reporting if and when the issue of usage is raised. It is the opinion of *The Survival Guide to SaaS Optimization* that representation of the business unit in the SaaS Governance Team reduces this gap and ultimately brings a 'plan achievement' perspective to the team which helps refine the SaaS Control Map (ESO Tool 2).

Before we leave the subject of Shadow IT, *The Survival Guide to SaaS Optimization* would like to address the subject of 'employee purchase' of SaaS applications. This is an area in which I have observed a significant disconnect between messaging from SaaS Management Platform providers and an executive view of this issue. Based on my experience working with executives, an individual employee purchase of a SaaS application is typically viewed as a control-breakdown and not the activity of Shadow-IT. When this dynamic becomes visible to the executive suite, there tends to be shock concerning the unmanaged risk exposure created by this practice. While SaaS-circles talk about employee experience and employee satisfaction, board members talk about regulatory judgments and reputation risk exposure.

Ultimately the value of a SaaS Management Platform will be to identify non-compliance for adherence to corporate SaaS policies and controls, holding the party accountable.

- **Cloud Center of Excellence:** The second misconception concerning an enterprise focus on SaaS governance and optimization is the role of a dedicated Cloud Center of Excellence. Many organizations established Cloud Centers of Excellence (CCOE) as a means to accelerate cloud adoption and speed their path to a digital future. Typically, within the IT infrastructure organization, CCOE's claim accountability for all things cloud, however Software as a Service capabilities are viewed as small, annoying tactical toys or labeled as shadow IT responsibilities. Again, leaving a SaaS governance void that enables risk and over-spending to grow unchecked.

  Enterprise CCOE's focus on moving infrastructure workload to the cloud and ensuring the approved architecture and solutions are adhered to. They have little to do with SaaS governance or any form of license use optimization activities. Organizations may think the CCOE is responsible for SaaS or perhaps the CCOE has created the impression they are involved, but reality shows this unfortunate misconception has led to a complete absence of any meaningful coordinated management of SaaS assets.

While this may change slightly with the continued growth of Enterprise SaaS services, *The Survival Guide to SaaS Optimization* projects the emergence of dedicated SaaS Optimization Office (SOO) as the most effective means to for a mid to large enterprise to govern and optimize their SaaS portfolio. As SaaS eclipses 40-50% of an organization's annual software spend and the unique characteristics of individual SaaS segments becomes clear, progressive firms have begun to see the value to invest in dedicated skills and function. I will expand on this concept in the next section as well as describe the evolutionary process by which SaaS governance progresses from the activities of the initial SaaS Governance Enablers to formation and engagement of the SaaS Governance Team ultimately progressing to a dedicated SaaS Optimization Office.

Part 1 Closure: SaaS Governance

Before leaving SaaS Governance, let's take a moment to summarize the key items that have been discussed.

- It is well documented the SaaS segment has grown dramatically with all forecast indicating no slowing in this phenomenon. As new offerings pour into the category, natural segmentation is occurring requiring organizations to reevaluate how they govern this increasingly complex category of SaaS applications to manage risk and establish the required governance strategy.

- Sourcing leaders are called upon to support governance and renewal activities for an ever-increasing number of SaaS agreements. These Sourcing leaders are in the best position to secure Chief Financial Officer (CFO) executive sponsorship and assemble a cross-functional team to develop a unified front for SaaS governance that addresses operational risk, vulnerability measurement and optimized spend.

- Governance, Risk & Compliance (GRC) leadership is an emerging executive function that can work collaboratively with the CFO and echo the need for close governance of SaaS partners to establish and maintain the necessary controls to satisfy regulatory requirements.

- Tool 1 of the Empowered SaaS Optimization (ESO) framework, Active SaaS Universe Roster, provides a simple means to track SaaS partners and several important data elements to produce insightful reporting and analysis. Use of this template will begin to bring transparency and visibility to the composition of you firms SaaS footprint.

- *The Survival Guide to SaaS Optimization* utilizes a 6 phase SaaS Life Cycle to provide an appropriate level of detail and depth to the issues and activities that emerge in each. This depth is captured in ESO Tool 2, the SaaS Control Map.

- ESO Tool 3 reviewed the 7 Core Activities of the SaaS Governance Framework. When aligned with the individuals representing members of the SaaS Governance multi-functional, multi-discipline team, we developed 2 unique SaaS Governance RACI's based upon SaaS segment groupings in the third tool of the ESO framework.

- Finally, *The Survival Guide to SaaS Optimization* calls out the value organizations will realize with the introduction of a dedicated SaaS Optimization Office (SOO). While this development has only begun to emerge, as the use of SaaS applications and capabilities continue to grow, as does the associated risk of these cloud-based services, SOO's will emerge as the most effective means to govern and optimize an organizations SaaS portfolio.

With SaaS governance defined, we are now ready to utilize the foundation established and move into the all-important activity of ongoing, effective optimization of SaaS services.

Part 2: SaaS Optimization

Congratulations! You have taken the time to understand the importance of establishing a comprehensive SaaS governance foundation before turning your attention to the issue of SaaS optimization. Now as we move into this important topic, we need to take a moment to carefully define what is meant by 'optimization' and the multiple dimensions SaaS Governance Enablers must consider to achieve true empowered optimization results.

At the outset of *The Survival Guide to SaaS Optimization*, I stated that the majority of organizations I have worked with define optimization as the **pricing concessions gained as part of a negotiation or renewal.** Sourcing, Vendor Management and other teams may be able to claim a win in this scenario, but this represents only a single dimension of true SaaS optimization. In many ways, SaaS provider account teams take full advantage of this common interpretation of SaaS optimization, keeping a clients focus away from detailed usage analysis and carefully growing the number licenses, premium license types and add-ons as a means to lock-in contract revenue growth.

As SaaS applications and offerings continue to expand with true enterprise capability, how a firm defines optimization must shift to include more elements and layers. Those SaaS partnerships that only deliver budget-friendly services or minimal business value will grow vulnerable to replacement. To emphasize this point, SaaS Governance Enablers, working with business and IT executives, have the opportunity to shape how the definition of SaaS optimization evolves over time.

In Part 1 of *The Survival Guide to SaaS Optimization* we defined SaaS segments, got a handle on the universe of SaaS applications and capabilities in our environment including the level of spend with each, created a multiple phase SaaS Control Map and defined the SaaS Governance Framework including core activities and the roles and responsibilities of the functional team involved with SaaS governance and optimization activities.

Now as we move into Part 2 of *The Survival Guide to SaaS Optimization*, we will focus on a few core areas necessary for SaaS Governance Enablers to achieve optimization success. These areas are:

- Establish a broad, multi-dimensional understanding of SaaS Optimization: <u>ESO Tool 4 – SaaS Optimization Decomposition</u>

- Define risk criteria by which each SaaS application will be assigned and monitored a risk designation: <u>ESO Tool 5 – SaaS Risk Categorization</u>

- Develop a program designed to deliver maximum SaaS spend efficiency across all SaaS segments: <u>ESO Tool 6 – SaaS Optimization Levers by Segment</u>

Optimization Decomposition

The goal of ESO Tool 4, SaaS Optimization Decomposition, is to facilitate discussions with executive sponsors, stakeholders and business unit leaders to consider multiple dimensions of SaaS optimization and the value the organization will realize by adopting a broader optimization definition.

Based on experience running these sessions, I have seen my client's executive sponsors quickly recognize the limit of their current thoughts on SaaS optimization and the potential business value to be realized by adopting a more comprehensive view of optimization. While so much focus today is on license harvesting and license type leveling, SaaS Governance Enablers will need to clearly establish how these activities will be addressed and then built-upon to address innovation, business enablement and potentially competitive advantage.

Optimization Decomposition Elements

The SaaS Optimization Decomposition template (ESO Tool 4) provides some recommended suggestions to get the team started, however I encourage SaaS Governance Enablers to feel free to utilize the language and issues most relevant to your organization. Based on the time you have taken to develop the 3 initial ESO framework tools, you will have great insight to the current environment and a potential path to guide sponsors and stakeholders to a more mature definition on SaaS optimization dimensions.

One way to look at SaaS optimization categories is to define them as items with 'above the line' benefit or impact, meaning they influence revenue growth and a firm's offerings, while others will be 'below the line', meaning they focus on efficiency, value realization and risk mitigation. I have found using this approach very helpful when speaking with executives as it enables them to quickly see there is potential value in SaaS governance and optimization activities beyond simply ensuring appropriate license count.

- **Above the Line Optimization Categories**

  o **Business Innovation** – A key measure for use of a SaaS application is the ability to help organizations deliver enhanced customer value. To date this benefit has primarily been realized by 'cloud-first', agile business models. However, with the emergence of Enterprise SaaS and the continued development of Industry SaaS platforms, this will begin to encompass traditional enterprises.

  o **Competitive Advantage** - Speed to market. Extension of supply and value chain. Rapid customer engagement for improved experience. SaaS capabilities and applications can be a key enabler in these areas.

  o **Digital Enablement** - Focus on digitizing current capabilities. Improved cycle time, close time, decision making clarity are all areas that can benefit an organization bottom-line.

Empowered SaaS Optimization - Tool 4

SaaS Optimization Decomposition

Optimization Category	Currently	In Next 12 Months	In Next 3 Years	Importance	Measurement	Executive Sponsor
Business Innovation	No		Yes	High	How will this optimization component be measured?	<NAME>
Competitive Advantage	Yes		Yes	Low		
Digital Enablement	Uncertain		Yes	Medium		
Innovation Incubator						
Business Resilience						
Risk Management						
Value Realization						
Dynamic Measurement						
Flexible Optimization						
<OTHER>						
<OTHER>						

SaaS Optimization Summary Statement

<ENTER>

SaaS Optimization

Decomposition

o **Innovation Incubator** - Mutual investment in the development of future capabilities and potential ability to invest. Can the SaaS capability springboard capability?

o **Business Resilience** – Does the utilization of a SaaS platform enhance stability and business continuity?

- **Below the Line Optimization Elements**

o **Risk Exposure** - Measurement and monitoring of potential risk introduced to corporate environment due to use of SaaS service

o **Value Realization** - Typically viewed as cost avoidance or the benefit realized by the base SaaS capability to harvest and repurpose SaaS licenses

o **Dynamic Measurement** - Dynamic reporting available in the SaaS portal, tenant or instance usage data enabling ongoing license type and volume efficiency.

o **Flexible Optimization** - Ability to optimize up or down dynamically or based scheduled frequency to maintain alignment with need and universe.

Optimization Decomposition Maturity

ESO Tool 4, SaaS Optimization Decomposition, also provides SaaS Governance Enablers the opportunity to develop a time line to achieve a greater more diverse definition of SaaS optimization. During conversations with executive sponsors and stakeholders it is important to review each category and explore potential timing of the category being added to the optimization agenda. This helps create a maturity timeline by which SaaS optimization effectiveness can be measured. I have found in facilitating these sessions that teams need to be careful to not attempt to have all categories as part of the initial effort. It is important to show growth, expansion and maturity over the defined timeframe so don't hesitate to have items in the 'Next 12 Months' or 'In Next 3 Years' categories.

Lastly, SaaS Governance Enablers should take advantage of the section titled 'SaaS Optimization Summary Statement'. The goal being to create a statement covering the current goals and objectives of SaaS optimization and the evolutionary time line in which additional optimization categories will be added to develop an overall mature SaaS optimization model. An example of a recent client's initial SaaS Optimization Summary Statement was, "current SaaS optimization efforts are focused on establishing accurate license baselines for each SaaS application in Enterprise, Hybrid and Industry Segments while creating the means to track potential emerging operational risk in the remaining segments that represent the largest population of SaaS applications".

I strongly recommend your SaaS Optimization Decomposition list of 'Optimization Categories' contains several items related to Third Party Risk Management, Governance, Risk & Compliance as well as Security Vulnerability Management. While these items may not be part of the current scope of SaaS optimization, and by reviewing these with executive sponsors and stakeholders, by proactively identifying this critical issue, SaaS Governance Enablers continually reinforce the value SaaS governance and optimization efforts will deliver. This alignment will be further reinforced with development of the next Empowered SaaS Optimization tool, SaaS Risk Categorization.

SaaS Risk Categorization

Saving money by negotiating a SaaS renewal is meaningless if a SaaS application exposes your business to unnecessary regulatory risk and cybersecurity vulnerabilities. SaaS governance and optimization efforts must achieve a careful balance between these two primary values.

Borrowing heavily from the Third Party Risk Management (TPRM) and Governance, Risk & Compliance (GRC) disciplines, Tool 5 of the Empowered SaaS Optimization (ESO) framework, SaaS Risk Categorization, features a customized risk-based assessment by which SaaS Governance Enablers will categorize a SaaS applications risk profile. The outcome of this effort will be definition of an appropriate level of monitoring and due diligence per assigned risk category to ensure emerging SaaS risk is quickly identified and mitigated.

If your organization has a TPRM or GRC function, they will be able to lead the effort to develop the criteria by which SaaS risk is to be based. In fact, there may be a GRC platform such as Archer or MetricStream that already has established corporate-wide third party risk classifications and the criteria that drive the risk calculation. If not, SaaS Governance Enablers have the opportunity to collaborate with members of the SaaS Governance Team and define SaaS risk dimensions as well as leveling of these risk criteria leading to calculation of a SaaS providers overall 'risk category'. I have found in my discussions with corporate executives they quickly understand the value of determining the level of risk due to their organizations SaaS portfolio as they are being questioned by their Board Members. Through implementation of ESO Tool 5, SaaS Risk Categorization, SaaS Governance Enablers enjoy significant visibility and acceptance with these corporate leadership by demonstrating their ability to think beyond simple cost reduction tactics.

Development of ESO Tool 5, SaaS Risk Categorization structure, is a means to help SaaS Governance Enablers focus appropriate attention to those SaaS providers who present operational risk and the specific risk area of concern. Development of ESO Tool 5 will also help the team evaluate policies, controls and requirements previously defined in the SaaS Control Map (ESO Tool 2) to determine if there is an opportunity to revise these items to support advanced identification of potential risk and minimization of current SaaS operational risk levels.

While the first challenge encountered by SaaS Governance Enablers will be identification of an accurate and complete SaaS universe to be continually recorded in ESO Tool 1, SaaS Active Universe Roster, the second challenge will be establishing common, enterprise-wide risk categories and the characteristics of risk that determine an assigned risk category. SaaS Governance Enablers need to support internal compliance organizations and adopt the pre-defined criteria and categories whenever possible. Discuss with your GRC leader if they can add a 'SaaS' category to their current reporting and consider establishing integration of the TPRM or GRC platform with the SaaS Management Platform using an application programming interface (API). This is an area that SaaS Management Platforms do not address in an automated fashion so SaaS Governance Enablers will need to rely on manually maintaining ESO Tool 5, SaaS Risk Categorization, and if possible, review and collaborate with internal risk or compliance teams.

If your organization does not have a dedicated GRC or compliance function, SaaS Governance Enablers can support the creation of enterprise risk criteria and categories for SaaS capabilities and applications; bringing greater visibility to the need for compliance and risk measures to be institutionalized across the organization.

SaaS Risk Criteria

Defining your organizations risk criteria is an additional opportunity to facilitate a cross-functional workshop in which SaaS Governance Team members and extended experts who can help prioritize the criteria most relevant to defining and monitoring risk. Once in draft form, SaaS Governance Enablers should review these risk criteria and risk categories with executive sponsors including the CFO, the senior most Sourcing executive and the executive assigned the compliance and risk agenda at your organization. This additional activity will help ensure an executive perspective is blended with the operational focus of the SaaS Governance Team.

In my client engagements, I am finding greater emphasis on data management issues and confirmation of information security policies that meet the standards established by my clients CISO. I will start the workshop with the following 10 items but find many times the list will be reduced to a core 7 or 8 criteria. Functioning as the Governance SaaS Enabler, I like to ask questions such as 'What area of risk is of greatest visibility to your corporate board or C-Suite?', 'Have you had any near-misses of late?', 'Is there a specific area you are concerned'. This usually gets a good discussion kicked-off!

- **SaaS Provider Segment:** Helps a compliance focused analysis begin to see where risk is most prevalent by segment. This has been defined in ESO framework Tool 1

- **Level of Spend:** It is important to understand the level of annual spend with the SaaS provider which will again point to where risk may be emerging. It is not uncommon to see low annual volume in functional and tactical SaaS segments having disproportionate risk. This has been identified in ESO framework Tool 1 and should be dynamically updated based on new orders to maintain accuracy.

- **Data Importance:** With SaaS services, there would be multiple categories to consider: Data location, data access, data type, data management practices etc. This is core to regulatory compliance and core to a regulator's investigation.

- **Data Access:** Define who, when and where data will be accessed to understand level of potential exposure and points of vulnerability.

- **Business Continuity/Disaster Recovery:** Compliance executives will tell you this is a key focus of regulators today for SaaS capabilities. Due to the vulnerability of SaaS services to cyber-attacks and potential ongoing financial viability of many SaaS services, ensuring an outage or shutdown does not adversely impact the ability to safely and securely support clients and core value chain operations.

Empowered SaaS Optimization - Tool 5
SaaS Risk Categorization

SaaS Provider Name	SaaS Provider Segment	Level of Spend	Data Importance	Data Access	BC/DR Impact	Roadmap Alignment	Potential Process Disruption	Level of Integration / Configuration	Switchability	Plan B Alternative Exist	Risk Category	Executive Sponsor
<Saas 1>												
<SaaS 2>												
<SaaS 3>												
<SaaS 4>												
<SaaS 5>												
<SaaS 6>												
<SaaS 7>												
<SaaS 8>												
<SaaS 9>												
<SaaS 10>												

SaaS Risk

Categorization

- **Roadmap Alignment:** Is this a SaaS service or application your organization will configure and customize to support business process or is it a one-off, tactical use?

- **Potential Process Disruption:** Would the outage of the SaaS application cause internal business disruption and/or impact customer experience?

- **Level of Integration and Configuration:** As SaaS services grow more integral to IT and business processes, does the client organization lose leverage due to high degrees of customization and configuration?

- **Switchability:** Level of effort to remove, disengage and move to a new alternative.

- **Plan B Alternatives:** Are there viable alternatives in the event the decision is made to terminate?

These are basic, foundational suggestions for SaaS Governance Enablers to consider. Each of the individual Risk Criteria should be assigned 'High-Medium-Low' in order to calculate the overall risk category assigned to be assigned to the specific SaaS application.

You will also notice there is an 11th item identified for inclusion in the SaaS Risk Categorization template: The Executive Sponsor. As we did in ESO Tool 1, the SaaS Active Universe Roster, it is important to continually link SaaS applications to an accountable executive in order to drive the necessary approvals for review, selection and implementation of a SaaS capability. Non-compliant SaaS applications discovered in the environment present a significant ongoing challenge for SaaS Governance Enablers and executive assignment helps add a bit of leverage when combined with effective and active executive sponsor support from the CFO or Chief Compliance Officer.

SaaS Risk Categories

Based upon the weighting assigned to each risk criteria, SaaS providers will be assigned to a corresponding risk category. Once again, this approach will be very familiar to SaaS Governance Team members from TPRM, VMO and GRC functions, but it also supports the needs of Information Security and Internal Audit. Assignment of the SaaS partner to a risk category will trigger a predetermined level of monitoring and due diligence to ensure proactive measures can be implemented before business operations or corporate reputation are adversely impacted. For those of you in regulated sectors, this process also develops the type of evidence regulators will require to ensure an organization has the appropriate compliance measures in-place.

When facilitating workshops on this item, I find teams have a tendency to want to painstakingly define weighting for each category, leading to lengthy discussions that ultimately have little effect on the final scoring or category assignment. As SaaS Governance Enablers, do your best to guide this conversation by assigning a priority to the identified task. Those of highest priority or perceived importance receive a slightly higher rating. In my experience teams quickly forget this dimension so don't over engineer it if at all possible.

The Survival Guide to SaaS Optimization suggest the following 5 categories. Based on my experience working with clients, I recommend the list of risk categories is kept to a logical, manageable number so the activity of assigning SaaS applications is a straight forward effort.

- **Potential SaaS Risk Categories:**

  o **Extreme** –SaaS partners in this area will require proactive ongoing monitoring and a level of due diligence through the use of spot audits to ensure resilience and stability. Typically, a small subset of overall SaaS universe.

  o **High** –Greater due diligence and ongoing monitoring is required. Use of SaaS Management Platform aligned with the Third Party Risk Management platform will enable more effective risk monitoring.

- o **Moderate** – The universe of SaaS partners in the moderate risk category will represent the largest portion of the environment. Risk monitoring will be primarily automated activities. Incorporate Social Media services to keep track of employee sentiment.

- o **Low** – Due to the nature of SaaS, this risk category will be tactical capabilities with no sensitive or customer information involved.

- o **Emerging** – SGT members need to carefully consider the potential growth, expansion and roadmap alignment of the SaaS providers capabilities in this risk category. evaluated and monitored.

Utilizing the information complied for the SaaS Active Universe Roster (ESO Tool 1), SaaS Control Map (Tool 2), SaaS Optimization Decomposition (Tool 4) and SaaS Risk Categorization (Tool 5), SaaS Governance Enablers have assembled valuable insight that will enable rapid identification of those SaaS applications and capabilities that present the organization potential strategic value. These assets also point to the relative size and complexity of each segment and potential levels of optimization to be achieved by diligent application of governance tactics.

With all of these steps accurately and completely produced, we are ready to focus on empowered optimization of your organizations SaaS application portfolio.

Empowered SaaS Optimization

The Survival Guide to SaaS Optimization has established that not all SaaS applications and services are equal. Organizations need to carefully determine which SaaS partners present the greatest optimization return and concentrate efforts accordingly. Utilizing the SaaS segments defined in the SaaS Active Universe Roster (ESO Tool 1) along with the additional data fields captured in this template, SaaS Governance Enablers can prioritize and align optimization activities to produce the greatest overall benefit for your organization.

Empowered SaaS Optimization is the strategy by which SaaS Governance Enablers apply the appropriate optimization levers to achieve optimal, maximum cost management results. Reducing both spend to formally record save as well as license harvesting to secure cost avoidance.

SaaS Optimization Levers

Many organizations view optimization as the single activity of securing rate concessions during renewal negotiations, missing the multi-dimensional aspect of SaaS cost. While SaaS has grown dramatically since the early days of salesforce, governance maturity and methodologies to optimize SaaS usage remains low. With pressure building to better manage spend and proactively manage risk, SaaS Governance Enablers must adopt a multi-level, multi-lever view of optimization. Aligning these levers by SaaS segment enables you to be highly efficient and focused, leading to positive overall optimization outcomes. ESO Tool 6, Optimization Levers by Segment, has been designed to guide SaaS governance professional's design their optimization strategy.

It is difficult to optimize when the level of spend with a SaaS partner is ineffectively tracked. This is an all-too-common challenge for IT, IT finance and Sourcing executives who are continually struggling to determine total spend for the category and total spend for a specific SaaS application. Utilizing the output of ESO Tool 1 (SaaS Active Universe Roster), Tool 2 (SaaS Control Map), Tool 3 (SaaS Governance Framework) and Tool 5 (SaaS Partner Risk Categorization), SaaS Governance Enablers have taken a large step forward to understand the extent of their SaaS universe and determine overall investment in this growing segment.

It is not uncommon for actual SaaS spend to be 30-40% higher than the amount initially defined in the Enterprise Agreement (EA) due to the addition of a stream of subsequent order documents. This unfortunate challenge puts Sourcing, Vendor Management and SaaS Governance Enablers in a compromised position to negotiate a favorable renewal. Implementation of a SaaS Management Platform combined with a SaaS application purchasing workflow that requires sign-off from Sourcing or SaaS governance combined with data pulled from SaaS application portals will produce an accurate, comprehensive study of spend for each SaaS partner. Utilizing this in-depth level of data, SaaS Governance Enablers will be able to produce multiple views of SaaS spend by partner to benefit efficient renewals, budget forecast and highlight potential areas of waste and process non-compliance.

As indicated in ESO Tool 6, SaaS Optimization Levers, there are multiple levers by which SaaS Governance Enablers can drive savings in addition to providing a complete and accurate definition of SaaS spend.

Lever 1 Optimization – Spend Analysis

Lever 1 Optimization activities for SaaS Spend Analysis occurs across all segments. To accomplish this, the SaaS Management Platform must be tied into purchasing systems to capture initial agreements as well as any add-on orders. This is an area where combination of a SaaS Management Platform, integration with Purchasing and Sourcing processes as well as the ongoing activities performed by SaaS Governance Enablers provides the greatest potential to capture +90% of SaaS spend activity. These activities include ongoing tracking of all purchase orders logged into the SaaS providers portal.

Lever 1 Optimization, SaaS Spend Analysis, creates the necessary transparency to establish the crucial baseline to manage SaaS spend and identify areas for potential optimization.

Empowered SaaS Optimization - Tool 6
Optimization Levers by Segment

	Enterprise SaaS	Hybrid SaaS	HCM SaaS	Industry SaaS	Functional SaaS	Task SaaS	Other
SaaS Providers by % of SaaS Spend	40%	15%	5%	20%	10%	5%	5%
SaaS Providers by % of SaaS Population	5%	5%	2%	20%	25%	30%	13%
Optimization Impact Potential	High	High	Moderate	Moderate	Moderate	Minimal	Minimal
L1 Spend Analysis							
L2 Access Usage							
L3 Feature-Component Usage							
L4 Service-Platform Utilization							
L5 Process Alignment							

SaaS Optimization Levers

By Segment

I want to take a moment to speak to the 'nay-sayers' among us about the importance of this first identified optimization lever. I have been in many meetings with IT finance and Sourcing leaders who roll their eyes when I discuss the importance of knowing their current SaaS spend. Yet it is these same executives who are stunned when they learn there are multiple contracts with the same SaaS provider and that add-on purchase orders represent a shocking portion of total spend, meaning their upcoming renewal will be substantially greater than anticipated.

Lever 2 Optimization – Access Usage

Lever 2 is the current default definition of SaaS optimization. This is the focus of SAM Management platforms today as they utilize a Single Sign On (SSO) platform to determine in a user has accessed his or her SaaS application with perhaps the capability to measure the length of time the SaaS application was open. While this is a solid step in the right direction, stopping at this point leaves significant potential license harvest opportunities undiscovered.

It is recommended Lever 2 Optimization occurs across all SaaS segments and SaaS applications in the corporate environment. Making use of a dedicated SaaS Management Platform is a must. However, SaaS Governance Enablers need to be clear with SaaS executive sponsors and stakeholders that to harness the full benefit of these powerful platforms, a dedicated staff is required. This will provide the necessary capacity to combine data sources and achieve deeper optimization outcomes.

As indicated in ESO Tool 6, there will be segments where due to the number of SaaS applications utilized, Lever 2 Optimization activity is sufficient.

Lever 3 Optimization – Feature/Component Usage

Lever 3 Optimization, Feature and Component Usage, is where the SaaS Governance Enablers focus on those SaaS applications prioritized by segment where deeper analysis can yield substantial levels of additional optimization to be realized. Currently, many of the SaaS Management Platforms are a bit challenged to effectively address this area. It is clear they have targeted the required capabilities on their platform roadmaps, however to achieve the required level of analysis to produce Lever 3 optimization, SaaS executive sponsors need to seriously consider the value of a dedicated SaaS governance and optimization staff. The combination of staff, SaaS Management Platform reporting, SaaS Application Portal reports and internal system generated reports produces the ability to perform true curated SaaS optimization. I have found this combination consistently delivers significant additional save and cost avoidance, more than justifying the incremental investment in staff.

Due to the level of effort and time required, it is recommended SaaS Governance Enablers utilize the SaaS providers assigned segment to fine tune which partners require this level of analysis.

Lever 4 Optimization – Service/Platform Usage

Lever 4 Optimization, Service and Platform Usage, is a growing area across Enterprise and Hybrid SaaS segments. As organizations embrace incremental services from salesforce, ServiceNow, Adobe's Creative Cloud, SAP and Oracle, SaaS Governance Enablers must anticipate significant opportunities to optimize. Many times, the initial use of these items such as storage, sandbox's or other development capabilities are provided as part of a bundle. Very quickly, these items become standalone line items on the next renewal with very real cost implications.

Like Lever 3, it is recommended dedicated SaaS analyst dig into the portal or tenant data to generate the analysis required to support an upcoming renewal and ongoing reporting requirements. This detailed analysis will help SaaS Governance Enablers work with the teams using the SaaS capability to review current use and explore if there are more efficient ways to contract for these services. Many of these items can be very expensive with material impact to a renewal. Documented usage is the only means to support internal resources and business owners who can fall prey to SaaS account managers looking to achieve their revenue target.

Lever 5 Optimization – Process Alignment

When supporting a client develop an optimization plan for their SaaS portfolio, I find it is not uncommon to discover significant gaps between internal processes that produce inflated license consumption, forcing unnecessary true-ups and potential security vulnerabilities. Alignment between SaaS license assignment, end user computing list of users currently in Active Directory, Information Security's add-delete processes and Human Resources add-delete process can cause significant delays in harvest opportunities or leave unidentified wastage.

SaaS Governance Enablers, utilizing the analysis conducted through the initial 4 SaaS optimization Lever's will begin to sense where process improvement opportunities exist. I have found that when a client has matured their SaaS governance capabilities to identify process improvement opportunities, they produce real benefit to multiple teams across the organization. In addition, SaaS Governance Enablers will be able to incorporate these learnings into the SaaS Control Map and supporting policies and controls, strengthening the overall SaaS governance framework workflow.

As discussed earlier in *The Survival Guide to SaaS Optimization*, if SaaS Governance Enablers have secured the executive sponsorship of the CFO or Chief Compliance Officer (CCO), any leverage required to close gaps and achieve successful alignment across operational processes should exist. If not, ongoing analysis with quantified financial impact of the process shortfall will highlight the challenge for sponsors and stakeholders.

SaaS Optimization by Segment

You will notice in Tool 6 of the ESO framework, Optimization Levers by Segment, there are 3 separate rows across the top, each designed to help SaaS Governance Enablers prioritize the level of effort and investment in optimization activities. The 3 identified SaaS characteristics are:

- **Percent of overall SaaS spend by Segment:** With a clear definition of spend by segment, SaaS Governance Enablers can concentrate their efforts to those segments that stand the potential for greatest optimization outcomes.

- **Percent of SaaS applications per Segment':** An understanding of the number of SaaS applications and partners in each segment will support development of a strategy to achieve optimal optimization based on the level of effort required. For example, Industry, Functional, Task and other miscellaneous SaaS platforms will be primarily optimized through automated efforts with some prioritized portal analysis based on compliance exposure or perceived operational risk.

- **Optimization Impact Potential:** SaaS Governance Enablers need to carefully consider where the greatest optimization outcomes will be achieved and apply resources accordingly.

The goal of the Empowered SaaS Optimization (ESO) framework is to consistently deliver outstanding results for your organization. However, the challenge faced by SaaS Governance Enablers is to align expectation with your organizations level of investment. As indicated in Tool 6, SaaS Optimization Levers by Segment, a fully functioning and integrated SaaS Management Platform forms the critical foundation for all optimization efforts. In addition, to deliver optimization realized by Levers 3,4 and 5, a dedicated team of SaaS professionals is required. I have had several clients use the visual for the 'Optimization Levers by Segment' to justify the purchase of a SaaS Management Platform and secure the resources to support curated optimization activities.

It is the opinion of *The Survival Guide to SaaS Optimization* that with sponsorship from the Chief Financial Officer or the Chief Compliance Officer or both, as an organization spend on SaaS services pass a perceived threshold, the need to invest in a dedicated team of resources expert in managing SaaS partners will become evident. In working with clients and my discussions with executives from SaaS Management Platform tool providers, creation of a dedicated SaaS function is slowly emerging.

Part 2 Closure: SaaS Optimization

Part 2 of *The Survival Guide to SaaS Optimization* covered a broad range of topics related to the concept of optimization, many of which were probably outside of your area of focus as we pushed beyond financial measures and introduced concepts that have the potential to deliver greater organizational value and reduced operational risk.

Before leaving SaaS Optimization, I want to again take a moment to summarize the key items that have been discussed in this critical section.

- I introduced the concept of SaaS Optimization Decomposition to help SaaS Governance Enablers look beyond cost save for additional areas of value they can deliver to the business. Tool 4 of the ESO framework, SaaS Optimization Decomposition, provides an excellent starting point for discussion across executive sponsors and stakeholders.

- We then moved to the critical area of third party risk management and the opportunity SaaS leaders have to align with internal compliance, risk and information security teams. Tool 5 of the ESO framework, SaaS Risk Categorization, provides an excellent base for collaboration with these important functions. If your organization does not have dedicated TPRM or GRC leaders, the issue of operational risk is top of mind to every executive team. This is an additional opportunity to demonstrate that governing SaaS assets has benefit beyond spend efficiency.

- We went deep into the 'Levers' by which optimization of SaaS assets can be applied to yield outstanding results. ESO framework Tool 6, Optimization Levers by Segment, illustrates the appropriate levers by SaaS segment so SaaS Governance Teams can focus and prioritize efforts to achieve outstanding results.

- Last, I want to highlight what I call the 'SaaS Optimization Divide'. Essentially the gap that exist between the ability of a part-time team to generate SaaS optimization results versus a dedicated team. I find when executives are only concerned with spend efficiency and save, they will gravitate to Levers 1 and 2 as the SaaS optimization solution. It is when executives identify the growing strategic nature of the SaaS applications in their environment combined with concern for compliance risk and security vulnerabilities that the decision to invest in order to generate Lever 3,4 and 5 optimization benefits comes front and center.

The Survival Guide to SaaS Optimization and the Empowered SaaS Optimization framework provide an actionable playbook for SaaS Governance Enablers to implement. Now we need the team!

Part 3 – The Case for a SaaS Optimization Office (SOO)

To realize true SaaS optimization, *The Survival Guide to SaaS Optimization* recommends organizations establish a dedicated SaaS Optimization Office (SOO). We have identified SaaS governance and optimization as a multi-discipline, cross-functional issue growing in strategic importance to most enterprises. Many times, it is Sourcing who is put on point to manage SaaS relationships by negotiating renewals or final shape of the contractual agreement, but as outlined previously, Sourcing, Vendor Management, Third Party Risk Management, Information Security and others have a very active interest in establishing effective SaaS governance. However, these key resources must focus on their core mission and are challenged to provide the focus necessary to support SaaS governance and optimization activities.

To establish and maintain SaaS governance and optimization best practices a dedicated team is required. The team must have a 'front-office' function to work across the many internal parties impacted by SaaS decisions combined with a 'back-office' function to generate the deep analysis on an ongoing basis to identify optimization opportunities and monitor emerging regulatory risk and security vulnerabilities.

Establishing a clear mission for the SaaS Optimization Office is a foundational requirement. SaaS Governance Enablers and executive sponsors must communicate the focus of the SOO is to support business units by providing central, expert governance activities designed to deliver optimized outcomes across an organization's portfolio of SaaS partners. This approach makes clear that technical evaluation, decision to select a SaaS application and ultimate ownership of the SaaS relationship remains with the business unit and their leadership. In addition, it must be clearly communicated that any optimization produced by the efforts of the SOO will benefit the business unit's budget and not be reclaimed or repurposed.

Establishing a dedicated SaaS Optimization Office (SOO) enables an organization to fully deploy the Empowered SaaS Optimization (ESO) framework delivering value at both enterprise and business unit levels. I have found executive leadership is receptive to the potential of establishing a dedicated SaaS Optimization Office team when overall SaaS spend begins to approach or exceed $20 million annually or there is growing concern of regulatory exposure and security vulnerabilities.

ESO Tool 1, Active SaaS Universe Roster, is a key asset for SaaS Governance Enablers to set the stage for the discussion about how to best govern this growing category. Until the size and growth of SaaS across the enterprise is documented, leadership will only suspect or intuitively sense potential risk. Once the data is presented, corporate leaders will be more aligned to take action with potential investment. The Empowered SaaS Optimization framework has been developed to deliver the necessary information on which to establish the dedicated SaaS Optimization Office.

SaaS Optimization Office Evolution

Emergence of a SaaS Optimization Office is in its infancy. While many within an organization have identified the challenge of effective SaaS governance, few have reached the point of taking proactive measures to establish an enterprise-wide, central SaaS governance and optimization capability. Currently, the default initial action is for a firm to consider investment in a SaaS Management Platform. I view this as extremely positive as those who adopt a platform will begin to see the incremental value. By adding dedicated staff, they will be able to produce additional levels of optimization and compliance due diligence activities.

Based on my direct experience working with Sourcing executives to assess and design SaaS governance and optimization strategies, I believe the ground swell is now beginning to occur where Sourcing leaders are intensifying their internal messaging concerning the value of post-agreement governance of SaaS services and value to be realized by implementing continual governance and optimization measures. These Sourcing leaders are seeing firsthand the challenge to effectively manage the SaaS category. Their initial attempts to add SaaS optimization and renewal responsibility as a sub-task to an existing team member is proving to be frustrating with little hard savings to point to as these associates are simply being overwhelmed by the volume.

In collaboration with IT finance and compliance leadership, Sourcing leaders once again have the opportunity to call out the need for a dedicated, central team of experts to continually monitor SaaS partners to drive optimization and risk identification. The Empowered SaaS Optimization framework is designed to help these leaders initiate the required focus on this emerging area of exposure.

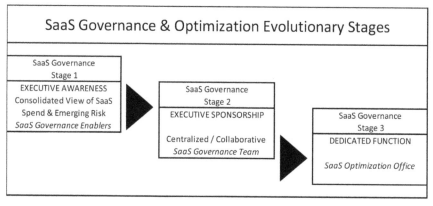

Figure 2: SaaS Governance & Optimization Evolutionary Stages

Properly implemented, the ESO framework creates transparency of an organizations SaaS footprint and guides SaaS Governance Enablers to implementation of the necessary measures to effectively manage SaaS assets. However, it is recommended these executives take small, incremental steps to build the business case to achieve the ultimate desired outcome: a dedicated SaaS Optimization Office that is self-funded will have the ability to deliver ongoing optimization of SaaS services while carefully monitoring and mitigating emergence of operational risk.

To achieve this goal, professionals focused on governing and optimizing SaaS assets must take an evolutionary approach, creating visibility with corporate executives of the expanding value to be realized by increased focus and investment.

Evolution Stage 1: Centralized SaaS Awareness

As the SaaS Governance Enabler, you create visibility and seek out others in the organization with a shared interest who will benefit from greater focus on effective governance and optimization of the organizations SaaS portfolio. *The Survival Guide to SaaS Optimization* has mentioned several likely candidates who can be powerful and influential partners, but every organization is different so use your judgment as you begin to explore potential allies.

In my corporate role, I was responsible for IT Vendor Management, IT First Line of Defense (FLOD) for Third Party Risk Management and Software Asset Management. While I was concerned about the emergence of SaaS and how it would impact my organization, it wasn't until I was questioned by my IT finance leader on how I was managing SaaS and tracking spend that I realized the issue was going to require proactive engagement. Shortly after this encounter, I was sitting with my IT Category Sourcing partner who shared he had just left a meeting with the CFO and there was growing concern about the ability to control SaaS usage across the global enterprise and potential regulatory implications. We quickly developed an outline for a SaaS Governance plan and secured the executive sponsorship of both our CFO and IT finance leader. Without realizing it, we acted as the SaaS Governance Enablers and with the strong endorsement of our CFO, were able to pull together a multi-functional team to develop SaaS policies, controls and the criteria by which SaaS capabilities would be assessed for appropriateness.

Empowered SaaS Optimization framework Tool 1, SaaS Active Universe Roster and Tool 2, SaaS Control Map are excellent templates to help SaaS Governance Enablers or a small group of professionals interested in SaaS governance begin the process to document the current size of the SaaS environment, prominent SaaS segments, business unit utilization and identify potential policy or control gaps. With this information documented, SaaS Governance Enablers should carefully consider the data and develop targeted messaging for those executives targeted to be SaaS governance and optimization sponsors. As part of these review sessions, I have found it very helpful to have a suggested SaaS Governance Framework (ESO Tool 3) based upon the insights gained during the process of gathering SaaS usage and governance data.

The goal for SaaS Governance Enablers is to secure support of executive sponsors to reach out to each of the leaders of the identified functional areas in the SaaS Governance Framework and ask if they would nominate one of their key staff to participate in a newly formed SaaS Governance Team. The request should clearly state the purpose of this team is to establish cross-functional collaboration to establish the basis by which SaaS assets will be controlled and monitored.

If the urgency and appetite to support a broader, cross-functional team is not endorsed by executive sponsors at this time, SaaS Governance Enablers should not get frustrated but continue to use the information from the first 4 tools of the ESO framework as a means to continually inform and educate the targeted executive sponsors and stakeholders. The goal of these ongoing communications being to provide transparency of the current SaaS footprint and trends, current state of SaaS policies and controls and their implications, and potential optimization dimensions that can deliver real business value.

At the minimum, by utilizing the initial tools of the ESO framework you have raised visibility of the growing SaaS footprint and the need for updated guidelines and workflows to review and approve SaaS adoption. In time, you stand the high probability of securing endorsement to form a SaaS Governance Team with each and every update provided to the targeted executive sponsors. Once again, I have seen great success when SaaS Governance Enablers target the CFO or Chief Compliance Officer with some level of support from the

Chief Information Security Officer (CISO) so make certain to explore multiple potential avenues.

Due to the ongoing tension and political dynamic between Information Technology and Shadow-IT resources across business units, I have found it more challenging for CIO's and IT leadership to establish the necessary independent platform to gain full support and acceptance as an executive sponsor from business unit owners. I don't mean to imply it impossible as every organization is different, however, I suggest SaaS Governance Enablers focus initially on the corporate executives identified, potentially viewing a CIO as a second-tier choice.

If the CIO is the executive sponsor, SaaS Governance Enablers need to be sensitive to potential resistance and take additional measures to assure business unit leaders the goal of the effort is to provide value, not control or pull budget.

Evolution Stage 2: SaaS Governance Team

Throughout *The Survival Guide to SaaS Optimization*, we have spoken about the SaaS Governance Team (SGT), identified logical member candidates and their motivation for participation in an effort to govern and optimize the organizations SaaS portfolio. With endorsement of the targeted executive sponsors, SaaS Governance Enablers who have stepped forward to promote the importance of creating a central, comprehensive SaaS function, can now assemble the targeted roles to form the SaaS Governance Team.

The primary benefits an organization will receive by establishing the SaaS Governance Team is creation of a blended perspective to establish comprehensive SaaS policies and controls to continually assess risk across the full SaaS Governance Framework while aligning internal processes to deliver new levels of SaaS governance and spend optimization.

Utilizing the Empowered SaaS Optimization framework, the SGT collectively reviews the Active SaaS Universe Roster to identify missing data points (ESO Tool 1) followed by detailed collaboration of the SaaS Control Map (ESO Tool 2) to establish the necessary workflow by which SaaS applications are evaluated and the criteria by which acceptance is determined. This is then followed by a review the stages defined in the SaaS Governance Framework and identified roles and responsibilities for those parties targeted for involvement (ESO Tool 3).

Once completed and all input and perspectives are incorporated, SaaS Governance Enablers facilitate a workshop with the SGT focused on the manner in which SaaS governance and optimization will be defined and measured. Utilizing the SaaS Optimization Decomposition template (ESO Tool 4), members can debate, challenge, add or delete identified optimization items, ultimately creating the definition of how your organization will control and assess optimization effectiveness of SaaS capabilities moving forward.

It is recommended the SGT meets on a monthly basis over which time the balance of the Empowered SaaS Optimization templates are workshopped with the members to create the comprehensive platform by which SaaS partners are governed and optimized. This includes SaaS Risk Categorization (Tool 5) and Optimization Levers by Segment (Tool 6). In addition, the SGT should meet quarterly with the executive sponsors to brief them on progress, opportunities and challenges to implementing governance and optimization measures.

The goal of the SGT is to create deep visibility to an organizations total SaaS footprint and the necessary activities to govern and optimize this rapidly growing and diversifying group of partners while identifying the risk associated with the services provided by SaaS partners and how they will be monitored and mitigated. For many organizations today, formation of an SGT will be the extent of investment to manage SaaS assets. In the current environment, I have found executives are hesitant to invest in a dedicated SaaS Optimization Office without validation of the benefits to be realized. Coordinated by SaaS Governance Enablers leveraging the assets of the Empowered SaaS

Optimization framework, a SaaS Governance Team will establish high visibility and clear documentation of the value realized due to the implementation of governance and optimization practices. In many cases, this level of spend optimization and risk monitoring is sufficient to make executives comfortable.

Ideally executive sponsors and stakeholders have realized the benefit and contribution of the effort to govern and optimize SaaS assets and are requesting additional recommendations from SaaS Governance Enablers to achieve greater results. This may take time to accomplish or it may be triggered due to a high-profile regulatory compliance judgment, but SaaS Governance Enablers should not become frustrated.

Formation of a SaaS Governance Team is a significant step forward for an organization. In fact, I have found organizations whose annual SaaS spend is less than $20 million and do not have a focus on regulatory risk or information security vulnerabilities, implementation of an SGT is the optimal approach to govern and optimize SaaS assets. Firms with SaaS spend at this level produce positive optimization outcomes when effort is focused on the first 2 levers of optimization as defined in the ESO framework's Tool 6, Optimization Levers by Segment, and a SaaS Management Platform is deployed and integrated with core internal systems.

Evolution Stage 3: SaaS Optimization Office

For those organizations with annual spend on SaaS services exceeding $20 million combined with an active regulatory and compliance corporate focus, establishing a dedicated SaaS Optimization Office (SOO) is an attractive solution. Tool 6 of the Empowered SaaS Optimization framework illustrates the multiple additional levers required to achieve and maintain true optimization across all SaaS segments.

Aligning the current SaaS portfolio by segment, spend and potential optimization levels enables SaaS Governance Enablers to develop the business case necessary to evolve the SaaS Governance Team from a group of interested, part-time team members to justify the launch of a dedicated SaaS Optimization Office.

Ultimately formation of the SOO is designed to help business units secure the best outcome for their investment in SaaS services, allowing them to redirect harvested budget to other areas they control. Leaders of the SOO will need to continually reinforce this message that any budget relief realized remains in that business units cost centers and demonstrate this to be the case. If business unit leaders suspect that the SOO is a central function whose focus is to reclaim their funding, the benefit of an SOO will be severely challenged.

First, value delivered by the SOO needs to be broadly defined. Tool 4 of the ESO framework, SaaS Optimization Decomposition, will help SaaS Governance Enablers and SOO leaders emphasize the value delivered to the enterprise and business units in terms beyond save or cost avoidance. Second, defining a clear mission for the SOO and reinforcing this mission with business unit leaders and their key operation stakeholders will reduce potential for passive aggressive political efforts to undermine the SOO. Visible and active support of the SOO's efforts by executive sponsors and stakeholders will also have a positive impact across business units.

SaaS Optimization Office Components

The opinion of *The Survival Guide to SaaS Optimization* is that a SaaS Management Platform is an enabler that supports a portion of a dedicated SOO's agenda, it is not THE agenda. SaaS Governance Enablers and SOO leaders need to continually reinforce with executive sponsors and stakeholders that it is the combination of Platform, People and Process that delivers true SaaS governance and optimization.

SaaS Management Platform

Due to the large number of SaaS products used in an enterprise environment, it is essential a SaaS Management Platform is utilized to dynamically discover SaaS applications and capture the volumes of SaaS usage data required to enable optimization activities. SOO leaders need to carefully define the expected value to be realized by implementation of a SaaS Management Platform and not communicate to executive sponsors that the tool is the 'end-all' solution to achieve optimization.

I have found this to be an unfortunate outcome of a SaaS Governance Enablers enthusiasm for justification of the investment in the tool. This led me to develop ESO Tool 6 as a means to provide a quick visual that sponsors and stakeholders can quickly see the value of the SaaS Management Platform but also the limits of the technology. While the tool will contribute heavily across all identified SaaS segments, it's the alignment with processes and the curated data analysis performed by a team of SaaS analyst that will drive optimization efforts beyond Lever 1 and Lever 2 savings. SaaS Governance Enablers need to be careful to avoid 'the guy and a tool' syndrome as this will ultimately lead to unmet executive expectations.

At this point it is important to understand the high-level categories vying for a piece of the SaaS Management Platform market. In an attempt to establish a simple classification, I place these tools in two basic groups: 'Fit for Purpose' and 'Module Extension'. While this may not be a perfect delineation, it covers the majority of current commercially available platforms.

- **'Fit for Purpose' SaaS Management Platforms** are net new tools developed by individuals with strong knowledge of the SaaS optimization challenge. As mentioned earlier, tools from this category can form a very productive foundation for a SaaS Optimization Office when combined with appropriate back-office analytical and reporting skills. A potential shortfall of these platforms is their SaaS-centric view of optimization with limited sensitivity to Compliance, Risk and Information Security. SOO leaders will need to carefully review Third Party Risk Management or Governance, Risk and Compliance integration capabilities to establish the desired broad, comprehensive governance and optimization mission of the SaaS Optimization Office.

- **'Module Extension' SaaS Management Platforms** are an attempt by existing tool providers to pivot and extend their platforms to include SaaS optimization capabilities. This segment is dominated by the traditional Software Asset Management platforms and IT Service Management providers. These too tend to only scratch the surface of SaaS governance and optimization due to a somewhat less native understanding of SaaS, however they will have stronger integration capabilities to support SaaS process alignment which I believe will grow more essential as the Enterprise SaaS segment grows.

- **Governance, Risk & Compliance / Third Party Risk Management** platforms are yet to make a push into the SaaS Management Platform segment, however with the continued increase of visibility on issues related to GDPR, PII and PCI implications of ungoverned SaaS applications with compliance executives, I am anticipating platform providers in this category to make a push.

To be sure, the SaaS Management Platform category is a rapidly evolving area and no clear winner has yet emerged. Based on my discussions with leaders of many of these firms, I am confident each tools capability will continue to be enhanced with additional Intelligent Automation (IA) capabilities. My guidance to SaaS Governance Enablers is to manage the expectations of your sponsors and stakeholders so they understand it is the combination of a dedicated team of professionals and the SaaS Management Platform that will produce consistent operational excellence.

SaaS Optimization Office Staffing (People)

At this point, I want to identify the core staff essential to deliver on the SOO charter and achieve the targeted governance and optimization benefits defined as part of the SaaS Optimization Decomposition template (Tool 4). An effective operational design for the SaaS Optimization Office must take into account which organization the SOO reports into, the level at which the SOO leader is slotted within this organization and careful assignment of the roles and responsibilities of SOO 'front-office' team members and 'back-office' analyst. Size of the staff will be directly dictated by current total SaaS spend and anticipated growth of SaaS applications across the enterprise.

- SaaS Optimization Office Reporting Structure

The first critical item to define is which organization will the SaaS Optimization Office report and at what level the leader of the SOO will be placed. In my dealings with clients, I have found the logical reporting path for a SaaS Optimization Office is first and foremost the Chief Financial Officer (CFO), followed closely by the Chief Compliance Officer or whomever in your organization owns the Governance, Risk and Compliance agenda. An additional alternative is the Chief Information Security Officer if they report directly to the board and are not reporting into the CIO office. If all else fails and the only executive willing to be executive sponsor of the SOO is the CIO, SOO leaders need to recognize the potential internal dynamics and take extra measures to ensure business unit leaders do not view the SaaS Optimization Office as an attempt to wrestle away autonomy or budget.

For those of you in the IT Asset Management and Software Asset Management professions you may not agree with my above recommendations. I do recognize that our European and Global partners have excellent operational visibility and will be viewed as strong candidates to own the SaaS optimization agenda, but in my experience, which is primarily North America, I do not find SAM or

ITAM teams have the necessary political leverage to drive an effective SaaS optimization outcome.

With alignment decided, the next crucial item is leveling of the SOO leader. Preferably the SOO lead would report directly to the executive, whether it be the CFO, Chief Sourcing Officer or Chief Compliance Officer. I have found this important as so many of the key stakeholders the SOO leader will need to influence are business unit executives and their operational leaders. By being a direct report to these highly influential executives, the SOO agenda has far greater visibility and perceived influence. However, as the function of SaaS governance and optimization is just now emerging, active and visible sponsorship by the executive sponsor will successfully support the SOO mission even with the SOO leader being leveled as a mid-tier manager within the organization.

- SaaS Optimization Office Leadership

I have found the typical structure for SaaS Optimization Office leadership is a single senior leader supported by 1 or 2 senior managers to provide the bandwidth to drive the extensive recommended front-office activities utilizing the Empowered SaaS Optimization framework. The SaaS Optimization Office must have a structure to effectively support 'front-office' activities across the organization supported by an analytical engine to perform 'back-office' analysis and reporting. In the initial stages, I recommend the leader is the first addition who then utilizes the core ESO templates the SaaS Active Universe Roster and the SaaS Control Map to initiate SaaS governance and optimization activities.

The size of the SOO 'front-office' team and the pace at which these associates are added will be based on the size of an organizations global SaaS footprint, emphasis on maintaining regulatory compliance and monitoring potential risk or security vulnerability exposure. I have found the individuals acting as SaaS Governance Enablers are able to quickly move into the role of SOO leader.

- SaaS Optimization Office Analyst

There is a significant level of analysis and reporting required for the SaaS Optimization Office to be effective. In addition to a SaaS Management Platform, data needs to be continually monitored and extracted from SaaS partner portals or tenants and compared with internal system generated reports including Active Directory user reporting, HR, InfoSec and others.

Analyst for these roles should be 'SaaS-aware' combined with a problem-solving perspective continually seeking to identify trends, issues and potential gaps. The number of analysts is dependent on the decision to invest in a SaaS Management Platform, the size and characteristics of the SaaS environment and the number of optimization items your organization has defined as optimal in ESO Tool 4, SaaS Optimization Decomposition. In combination with Tool 4, the SaaS Active Universe Roster (ESO Tool 1) and SaaS Control Map (ESO Tool2) are excellent resources to help determine the number of analysts that will be necessary to achieve the desired coverage. Currently, I am finding that a team of 2-3 dedicated analyst is sufficient to execute the ESO framework if they are supported by a properly implemented SaaS Management Platform, are provided direct access to the assigned SaaS portals in order to access usage detail and the internal system generated reports are produced on a predetermined schedule and provided to the team at the assigned time.

An important element to consider when developing the SaaS Optimization Office business case is the decision to hire dedicated resources to serve as the back-office function or explore the potential to use a managed service. Much like we have seen in other areas such as vendor management, software asset management, telecom expense management and third party risk management, SaaS optimization managed services are beginning to emerge. Currently, these services are relatively new and focused exclusively on Lever 1 and Lever 2 optimization measures, however I anticipate rapid maturing and expansion of these capabilities, providing SaaS Governance Enablers a viable alternative for consideration. If your optimization measures include compliance, risk and security vulnerability elements, SaaS managed services will be challenged to match the effectiveness of a dedicated internal team. Again, ESO Tool 4, SaaS Optimization Decomposition can serve as an excellent guide to support the direction you decide.

It is also important to note I am observing SaaS optimization managed services provide their capability on a percent of save or cost avoidance basis. This will enable SOO leaders to demonstrate to executive sponsors and stakeholders a solid return-on-investment for SaaS governance and optimization operations.

SaaS Optimization Office Operational Execution (Process)

- SOO Front-Office Activities

The Empowered SaaS Optimization framework provides an excellent roadmap for SOO leaders to establish an effective governance and optimization operation. The primary focus has been to create comprehensive visibility of SaaS utilization across the enterprise including operational risk, monitoring of security vulnerabilities and roadmap alignment to deliver true optimization. With the formation of a formal, dedicated SaaS Optimization Office, the Empowered SaaS Optimization tools now transition from creating transparency of your organizations SaaS application portfolio to guiding the operational strategies and tactics that deliver value.

Core SaaS Optimization Office 'front-office' activities include:

- o Business Unit Interaction
- o SaaS Strategic Partner Program Management
- o SOO Steering Committee Management
- o Sourcing Renewal Support
- o Third Party Risk Management/Compliance Support
- o Information Security (InfoSec) Support

- o   IT Finance Support

- o   Policy & Control Enforcement

- •   SOO Back-Office Activities:

Providers of SaaS Management Platforms have done a good job of highlighting the challenges faced by enterprises as their SaaS footprint continues to grow. However, these tools are completely focused on Lever 1 and Lever 2 license optimization with little insight to the issue of protecting a firm's operations from SaaS third party risk or compliance exposure. While these tools are an enabler, a SaaS Management Platform in and of itself is not the answer to achieve SaaS governance and optimization. SaaS Optimization Office leaders must be careful to avoid the 'guy and a tool' syndrome and falling short of executive expectations.

While I believe utilization of a SaaS Management Platform is a must, it is the combination of an effectively integrated SaaS Management Platform and a team of focused analyst that enables the SOO to effectively execute 'back-office' activities which include:

- o   SaaS Application Discovery

- o   SaaS Portal Report Generation

- o   Schedule/coordinate internal system generated reporting

- o   SaaS Usage & Optimization Analysis

- o   SaaS Partner Monitoring & Alerts

- o   InfoSec Report request

- o   Reporting & Trend Communications

- o   Renewal Support

- •   Back-Office Alternatives

The Survival Guide to SaaS Optimization recognizes the concept of a dedicated SaaS Optimization Office is just now emerging across enterprises. A key contributor to the growing interest in this area is the number of SaaS Management Platform providers now offering managed service capabilities, educating potential clients of the need to augment the tool with additional capabilities to deliver deeper optimization and governance outcomes.

 With an organizations decision to invest in a central SaaS governance and optimization capability, SaaS Governance Enablers will need to consider the 'buy vs. build' decision to establishing the SOO back-office capability as a core part of the business case.

    o   Dedicated Staff

I have found in my discussions with clients and their executives who have focused on the issue of SaaS governance that the role of SaaS Optimization Analyst is beginning to slowly emerge. A primary reason for this trend is the simple fact that Sourcing team members are hard pressed to effectively manage renewal optimization of SaaS services as part of their category management assignment. Using Sourcing's challenge, SaaS Governance Enablers need to carefully align the required skills of SaaS Optimization Analyst with the composition of the organizations SaaS portfolio by SaaS partner segment.

The advantage of a dedicated full-time staff is it facilitates collaboration across internal data sources incorporated into analysis of SaaS governance and optimization such as Sourcing, Purchasing, Third Party Risk, Finance, InfoSec and Compliance. It is this blended focus that ultimately leads to true optimization aligned with your organizations SaaS optimization definition documented in ESO tool 4, SaaS Optimization Decomposition.

    o   Managed Service

Utilization of a SaaS Management Platform's managed service offering or a third party's managed service capabilities will primarily focus the SaaS Optimization Office's efforts on Lever 1 and Lever 2 base optimization activity as described in ESO Tool 6, Optimization Levers by

Segment. Currently, *The Survival Guide to SaaS Optimization* believes these offerings are immature, but believe they will mature quickly.

I have found in conversations with the organizations providing these services today a 'SaaS-centric', 'tool-focused' approach to optimization. Meaning these services will purely focus on SaaS Management Platform output, many times missing the additional insight and optimization opportunities to be realized by extracting data from the assigned SaaS application portals. An additional weakness for most SaaS optimization managed service offerings currently is they miss a collaborative and close alignment with your internal risk, compliance, InfoSec and IT finance teams. This activity will need to be fully assumed by the SOO front-office team.

It is anticipated the SaaS Management managed service category will go through rapid expansion and change in 2021. SOO leaders need to monitor development of these capabilities and continually explore a 'value for money' analysis.

SOO Executive Steering Committee

As a new organization and internal capability, SOO leaders will realize significant benefit by establishing an Executive Steering Committee (Exec SteerCo) comprised of business unit leaders and leaders of the key functional areas we have identified such as InfoSec, Compliance, TPRM, VMO, Sourcing, IT Finance, Privacy and IT. Successful management and engagement of the SOO Exec SteerCo provides SOO leaders several very positive outcomes including:

- Continually reinforce the value and contribution of the SOO with key leaders. These individuals will carry that message with them when in other executive of unit specific sessions.

- Members provide a direct link to leaders of their operational teams. This is of great value when it is important for a message to be 'cascaded' throughout the organization or when an escalation is required.

- Exec SteerCo members will be able to intercede in their team's decisions to implement a SaaS application outside of the prescribed controls and re-direct them to the appropriate policy and control workflow

SOO leaders need to develop an appropriate plan to continually engage and inform the members of the SaaS Executive Steering Committee as they will be a valuable link to business operations. I offer the following guidance to support SaaS Governance Enablers and SOO leaders succeed in successfully engaging Exec SteerCo members:

- Make certain reporting and analysis is clear, direct, brief, to the point and addresses the interest of the members

- Hold formal quarterly review sessions with specific agendas defined and circulated in advance along with any analysis to be shared

- Use monthly e-mail status to keep the team informed

- Hold one-on-one sessions to ensure alignment with the current needs of members ongoing

In Part 4, we are going to cover in greater detail the measures by which SaaS Governance Enablers and SOO leaders can establish and maintain strong executive alignment with sponsors and stakeholders to ensure expectations are continually met.

Part 3 Closure: The Case for a SaaS Optimization Office: SOO

Part 3 of *The Survival Guide to SaaS Optimization* highlights the emerging trend of organizations to establish a consolidated, central function to govern and optimize their growing SaaS portfolio. Implementation of this capability tends to occur along a predictable evolutionary path where a small group of operational leaders (SaaS

Governance Enablers) successfully gain executive sponsorship. These executive sponsors endorse formation of a cross-functional, multi-discipline team (SaaS Governance Team) to collaborate and develop SaaS governance and optimization best practices utilizing the Empowered SaaS Optimization Framework.

Based on visible success and documented value delivered, SaaS Governance Enablers work with the SaaS executive sponsors and stakeholder to develop the business case for a full-time organization (SaaS Optimization Office) that is comprised of a 'front-office' team supported by a 'back-office' team of analyst to generate the ongoing SaaS governance and optimization reporting and communications that documents the benefits of governing and optimizing the rapidly growing SaaS portfolio.

Finally, with formation of the SaaS Optimization Office, SOO leaders engage a group of business and operational leaders to form the SaaS governance and optimization Executive Steering Committee (Exec SteerCo) to ensure continued alignment across the organization.

I want to impress upon you a couple of quick points before we proceed to Part 4, SaaS Optimization Office Executive Alignment:

- SaaS Governance Enablers need to take advantage of whatever point your organization chooses to start! The ESO framework will support your efforts regardless of SaaS governance maturity or the level of focus at your executive level. Don't worry, visibility of the issue and risk will emerge. Your efforts will position you well to be viewed as a proactive solution to the challenge: the SaaS Governance Enabler.

- Don't be concerned if the SaaS governance and optimization solution 'gets stuck'. Continue to report analysis utilizing the ESO framework tools and facilitate discussions on the value to be realized with true, multi-lever SaaS governance and optimization.

Now we turn our attention to the activities necessary to establish and maintain ongoing alignment with the SaaS Optimization Office executive sponsors and stakeholder. This is crucial to ensure the ongoing viability of the SOO!

Part 4 – SaaS Optimization Office Executive Alignment

Part 4 of *The Survival Guide to SaaS Optimization* provides SaaS Governance Enablers guidance on developing the alignment necessary with executive sponsors and stakeholders to ensure operational execution meets and exceeds expectations. I have found SaaS Governance Enablers suffer from the same tendency as other functions such as Vendor Management, Software Asset Management or Third Party Risk Management: the desire to quickly select a tool and initiate operations with no real understanding of executive expectations or the measures of success by which value will be assessed. The ESO framework now turns the focus to help SaaS Governance Enablers develop clear alignment with executives through collaboration of the SaaS Optimization Office Mission and Value Statements.

Empowered Executive Engagement

Before we discuss the strategy and tactics to establish and maintain effective executive sponsor and stakeholder engagement, I need to take a moment to stress the importance of these activities for SaaS Governance Enablers and your ability to secure the needed support. I know many of you will skip over this section or will quickly scan the recommendations while rolling your eyes, however I can assure you these simple, basic steps will pay tremendous dividends to the ongoing success of your SaaS governance and optimization efforts.

I have found clients who have engaged me to assess and design their SaaS governance and optimization function typically have a significant disconnect between the ultimate goals and objectives of the effort when I am speaking with executive sponsors versus those selected to run the operation. To remedy this situation and help establish a common expectation, I have used the following tools and tactics with great success. So please don't skip ahead! As you review this information consider who you should engage in these discussion and how you will communicate the SaaS Optimization Office charter to ensure expectations are aligned.

Sponsor Management

The Survival Guide for SaaS Optimization has repeatedly pointed to the CFO, Chief Procurement Officer and Chief Compliance Officer as the logical executives most likely to provide powerful and visible sponsorship of the SaaS governance and optimization agenda. As these executives can be challenging to gain access to consistently, SaaS Governance Enablers should focus their efforts to secure sponsorship of a direct report to these executives, however I have found in my dealings with clients, concerns regarding risk associated with SaaS usage are top of mind with executives. If properly prepared using the documentation you have created using the ESO toolkit, there is high probability you will secure the support necessary to kick-start a formal SaaS governance and optimization effort.

I provide the following to help structure these important initial interactions.

- **Sponsor Identification**: Is your organization most focused on regulatory compliance, environment vulnerabilities or budget management? This insight will help you target messaging for the targeted executive team member. We talked previously about the value of a close partnership with IT Finance, Third Party Risk Management and Sourcing. Representatives from these operations can provide great insight to the dynamics they observe when in closed-door executive sessions. Don't forget to engage leaders from the Vendor Management organization as well. Depending on your organization, Vendor Management may be parallel to the Sourcing team and reporting into the CPO as well.

- **Sponsor Engagement**: In combination with the data compiled in the ESO framework tools, explore the key types of information, insight and intelligence of greatest value to the targeted executive sponsors. Develop the means to report and update executive sponsors in these areas to ensure the reporting provided by the SaaS Optimization Office is on target, of value and aligns with expectations

- **Sponsor Expectation**: ESO Tool 4, SaaS Optimization Decomposition, is an excellent guide for a conversation with executive sponsors to determine how success will be judged. This insight will be invaluable to SaaS governance professional and should be reviewed frequently with sponsors and stakeholders to confirm the SOO measures of success remain consistent with any shifts noted.

Stakeholder Management

The Survival Guide to SaaS Optimization identifies 'stakeholders' as a separate group of critical professionals who hold a high degree of influence over the ability of SOO leaders to achieve success. For clarity, Stakeholders represent the critical link between executive messaging with on the ground operational support and execution. The majority of individuals targeted as Stakeholders will be direct reports to the Executive Sponsors or peers in other aligned areas.

We have identified multiple functional areas that can benefit from a central SaaS governance and optimization function. These disciples have been identified and engaged through development of the SaaS Governance Team based on the endorsement of our executive sponsors. SaaS Governance Enablers need to utilize this endorsement and work across the organization to develop alignment with these key operational leaders who will form the SaaS Stakeholder universe. Many of these individuals should be prime targets for inclusion in the ongoing SOO Executive Steering Committee.

- **Stakeholder Identification**: While every organization is different, there are some common functional areas important for SaaS Governance Enablers to make certain are engaged, informed and supportive. IT finance, Sourcing, Third Party Risk Management (TPRM) and Governance, Risk & Compliance (GRC), Information Security, Privacy, Software Asset Management, Vendor Management and others form a broad list of important stakeholders who will benefit from effective, centralized SaaS governance.

- **Stakeholder Engagement**: Utilizing the ESO framework tools as the basis for conversation, SaaS Governance Enablers can demonstrate the level of reporting, analysis and proactive measures intended for the SaaS Optimization Office. Understand how the intended reporting aligns with the stakeholders needs and identify any gaps that can closed will provide ongoing value.

- **Stakeholder Expectation**: As we did with sponsors, use ESO Tool 4, SaaS Optimization Decomposition, to drive a clear understanding of how success will be judged and discuss the progression of various optimization levers to continually advance the SaaS Optimization Office agenda.

SaaS Optimization Office: Charter

Many internal organizations struggle to realize their full potential as leaders are pressured to execute and achieve immediate operational execution. While the Empowered SaaS Optimization framework and supporting tools carefully guide SaaS Governance Enablers through a comprehensive methodology, there is still tremendous benefit to be realized by taking formal actions to develop, document and continually communicate the SaaS Optimization Offices operational Charter. The goal being to establish and maintain alignment with corporate objectives and the expectations of key executive sponsors and stakeholders.

With formation of a dedicated team to implement ongoing SaaS governance and optimization activities, it is critical for SOO leaders to invest the time and energy to develop a clear, concise Mission Statement as expectation can shift, causing dangerous misalignment with sponsors and stakeholders. The ESO framework has helped SaaS Governance Enablers develop comprehensive understanding of the issues and challenges presented by an organizations SaaS portfolio. This insight and intelligence can now be blended in the development of a compelling message and concise SaaS Optimization Office 'elevator pitch'.

- Mission Statement

A quality Mission Statement address the 'why', 'how' and 'when' the SaaS Optimization Office will deliver governance and optimization success. ESO Framework Tool 7, SaaS Optimization Office Mission Statement Framework, provides a simple template to assist SaaS Governance Enablers collaborate with sponsors and stakeholders to finalize an appropriate mission statement that reinforces the goals, objectives, expectations, authority and accountability of the SaaS Optimization Office.

- Value Statement

Perhaps the most challenging thing about creating a Mission Statement is to keep it brief, focused and effective. Too many times I have seen SaaS Governance Enablers experience 'mission statement-sprawl', projecting to sponsors and stakeholders a convoluted message and lack of focus. To minimize this urge to cover it all in a single statement, *The Survival Guide to SaaS Optimization* recommends the development of a separate SaaS Optimization Office 'Value Statement'.

A Value Statement is an equally important document that defines the dimensions by which value will be delivered and the specific

SaaS Optimization Office (SOO)
Mission Statement Framework

Empowered SaaS Optimization	Content	Guidance
Tool 7		
Mission Statement		It is important SOO and SaaS Governance Team leaders look beyond basic definitions of governance and leverage Tool 4 of the ESO to establish multiple optimization and governance dimensions. This forms the foundation of the SOO Mission and **WHY** the organization exist. *The Survival Guide to SaaS Optimization* suggest a Mission Statement that extends beyond spend optimization and efficiency to highlight the additional benefits in risk and compliance associated with SaaS services as well as enhanced process efficiency, environment optimization and overall IT spend that can be garnered from SOO insight.
Execution Statement		The opportunity to explain **HOW** the SOO will accomplish the Mission Statement. Speak of SaaS Controls, Polices and efforts to establish complete and accurate universe... Introduce the value to be realized through SaaS analysis and trending in addition to monitoring activities that support compliance and risk measures.
Optimization Measures		Highlight the optimization progression that has been defined using the SaaS Optimization Layers defined in Tool 4 of the ESO. The goal is to outline **WHEN** SOO operations will produce the desired outcomes, reporting cycles, non-compliance communications.
Shared Intelligence		The philosophy and approach for the SaaS Optimization Office has been to engage all functional areas, their operational leaders and their executives who not only benefit from SOO efforts but broaden governance, monitoring and optimization efforts.

SOO Mission Statement
Development

SaaS Optimization Office (SOO)
Value Statement Framework

Empowered SaaS Optimization Tool 8	Content	Guidance
Value Statement		SaaS governance professionals need to align 'value' with the current state optimization focus. Value for SaaS Optimization Office can be aligned in 3 broad buckets. Spend, Risk Avoidance and Mitigation, Vulnerability Reduction. Each of these areas will have sub-categories that are most relevant and aligned to your sponsors and stakeholder expectations.
Execution Alignment		Utilizing the ESO framework input from Executive Sponsors and Stakeholders, take the time to align their stated expectations of value with the focus and actions of the SOO.
Outcome Produced / Contribution		Next, be specific about how value will be measured, documented and reflected in the IT finance or business unit budget.
Manner Communicated		SOO leaders need to carefully, effectively and consistently deliver reporting for executive consumption aligned by the value areas identified above. Ensure to communicate and track value ongoing. Do not assume the message is getting thru to the intended audience! Repeat, Repeat, Repeat

SOO Value Statement

Development

metrics by which success will be measured. The ESO framework Tool 8, SaaS Optimization Office Value Statement Framework is an excellent guide to help SaaS governance and optimization leaders develop this essential messaging. Using Value and Mission Statements in tandem form an important combination that ensures SaaS Optimization Office activities remain aligned and reinforced with sponsor and stakeholder expectations.

SaaS Optimization Office: Visibility

The Empowered SaaS Optimization framework is designed to help SaaS Governance Enablers establish and maintain maximum visibility with executive sponsors and operational stakeholders. Leaders of the SaaS Optimization Office need to continually monitor reception to the reporting and analysis to identify fatigue on the part of the intended audience. Many times, new teams will overwhelm their intended audience with volumes of data only to produce confusion or frustration with recipients. As the ESO framework tools have been customized through collaborative workshops with targeted executives and operational leaders, SaaS Governance Enablers have had the opportunity to identify and prioritize the actions by which the SOO will achieve visibility. In addition, by virtue of leading these sessions, SOO leaders have established a leadership role with important connections across the organization's executives.

There are a few key tactics that will ensure visibility of the SaaS Optimization Office while continually reinforcing delivery of the Mission and Value statement expectations.

- **Succinct Reporting:** Through implementation of the ESO framework, combined with SaaS discovery analysis from the SaaS Management Platform integrated with key internal processes, there will be no shortage of data to produce deep, insightful analysis. The challenge will be

SOO leaders need to develop a roadmap outlining the stages of reporting illustrating the careful expansion of analysis. In this manner, executive sponsors will be able to help prioritize and sequence items based on their needs.

- **Clear Communications:** With reporting and analysis to be produced by the SaaS Optimization Office defined, it is critical to develop a multi-faceted, multi-tiered communications strategy. This needs to include timing, roll-out of the information and levels of analysis depth. SaaS Governance Enablers should use a 'ground-up' approach, creating the detailed in-depth analysis appropriate for an operational team and then extract the key summary points for an executive summary with targeted recommendations.

- **Predictable Schedule:** The truth is everyone has far too many meetings and demands for their time. SaaS Governance Enablers need to consider the appropriate level of meetings with sponsors, stakeholders and the SaaS Executive Committee. Find a balance to ensure each audience is continually informed while not dominating their calendar.

In follow-up meetings with my clients, I have observed many teams become enamored with data analysis, almost completely withdrawing from the activities to promote and strengthen the vision of the SaaS Optimization Office. Be careful to avoid this 'back-room syndrome' and be visible! Don't rely on hitting the 'send button' as your primary communications platform.

Part 4 Closure: SOO Executive Alignment

The goal of Part 4, SaaS Optimization Office Executive Alignment, was to help SaaS Governance Enablers visualize how to best engage and align with executive sponsors and operational stakeholders. Development of the SaaS Optimization Office Charter, inclusive of Mission and Value Statements, enables SaaS Governance Enablers to achieve long-term success by ensuring expectations are continually aligned across sponsors and stakeholders.

The Survival Guide to SaaS Optimization and the Empowered SaaS Optimization has taken SaaS Governance Enablers through the detailed framework by which you establish effective SaaS governance and optimization practices. In Part 5, I share with you the methodology I have applied multiple times to guide clients through the implementation of the ESO framework to achieve outstanding results.

Part 5 – ESO Framework Methodology Implementation

So far, we have reviewed a total of 8 individual tools that comprise the Empowered SaaS Optimization framework. Before I bring *The Survival Guide to SaaS Optimization* to a close, I want to share with you the methodology I utilize when implementing the ESO framework with clients and share with you the last tool of the ESO framework which is designed to provide ongoing benchmarking of your SaaS governance and operational maturity. In addition, I want to share some of the typical dynamics I encounter when working with clients to help you visualize the steps and flow of implementing the ESO framework that will work best for your specific situation.

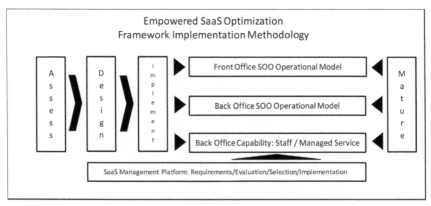

Figure 3: ESO Implementation Methodology

ESO Methodology Implementation Components

I have developed a simple implementation methodology to help you successfully apply the Enterprise SaaS Optimization framework and the 9 core templates in a logical sequencing. My goal is to help you answer the questions:

- How do I get started and help my organization bring focus to this important issue?

- Where will potential opportunities and challenges emerge?

- How do I support continued maturing of current SaaS governance and optimization activities?

I thought the best way for me to offer guidance is to share the steps and activities I employ when preparing to engage with a new client. I have had great results applying this simple, straightforward approach with clients regardless of where they are on their SaaS governance and optimization journey. I'm still a 'hard-copy' person so I like to have all the templates out and viewable so I can ensure I capture all the relevant data points as I consider development of my interview guides. I do this in advance of engaging with the client and initiating the methodology captured in Figure 3.

Before I formally start my assessment of the clients SaaS governance and optimization readiness and have fully developed the interview guides, I make certain to put myself in 'SaaS Governance Enabler-mode'. By assuming this role and leveraging the ESO tools, I am able to fully appreciate the opportunities and challenges an organization will encounter on the path to establishing a productive SaaS governance and optimization capability that is endorsed and supported across an organization. I ask you now to put yourself in the SaaS Governance Enabler mindset as we review the ESO implementation methodology.

Assess

In preparation for the initial activity to implement the ESO framework, I create a series of questionnaires to use as a discussion guide for meetings with potential executive sponsors and key operational stakeholders of a potential central SaaS governance and optimization capability. As the SaaS Governance Enabler, we are looking to see which of these executives may be willing to serve as an executive sponsor and stakeholder to support ongoing SaaS governance and optimization activities. I will use these discussion guides as well for my interactions with corporate executives with the goal of identifying the unique expectations of each of these 3 distinct groups. As I gather my thoughts, I will have hard copy of the following ESO tools so I can ensure to highlight key areas and sequence the questions to facilitate a full and open dialogue.

- **SaaS Active Universe Roster (Tool 1):** I will use this template to ensure I get a sense of current focus on SaaS governance. Does the client have a segmentation approach? Do they track spend? If yes, is it believed to be accurate? Do they track SaaS activity by business unit, noting the executive sponsor? Is SaaS spend budgeted at the business unit, cost center level or are cost passed to IT?

- **SaaS Control Map (Tool 2):** With the basics understood, I want to turn the conversation to understand if the client has taken the time to develop dedicated SaaS policies and controls and what measures have been put in place to govern and track risk exposure? It is typically in this portion that the leaders I am speaking with begin to realize that a fixation of SaaS spend management ignores the emerging risk and vulnerabilities poorly governed SaaS portfolios contain.

- **SaaS Optimization Decomposition (Tool 4):** Now that we have broached the concept of risk and vulnerabilities, I like to use the SaaS Optimization Decomposition list of items to reinforce the comprehensive potential true optimization can provide their organization. It is at this time I continually observe executives begin the process of shaping strategies to mitigate risk in their environment that perhaps was not previously considered.

- **SaaS Risk Categorization (Tool 5):** With the focus now on risk and vulnerabilities, I turn the conversation to review current internal measures concerning regulatory compliance, privacy and overall, third party risk practices. Typically, I am asked to follow-up this discussion with multiple additional meetings with corporate executives as the realization that SaaS services introduce untold risk and exposure begins to become clear.

- **SaaS Optimization Levers by Segment (Tool 6):** Before I bring the discussion to a close, I want to change the focus of the meeting to understand the executives view of the level of expected optimization and an appreciation for the level of effort and investment necessary to achieve true optimization.

Depending on the size of the organization, I typically target 10 – 12 executive and senior leader meetings. One quick note, as you will see from the above, I do not ask about technology tools or platforms. My goal is to reinforce the comprehensive, multi-functional requirement to establish credible SaaS governance and optimization capabilities. If I am asked by the individual about a SaaS Management Platform, I reinforce the opinion that the tool is an enabler to a SaaS governance solution but it requires the appropriate investments in manpower, polices and controls and process alignment to deliver the desired outcome.

Before initiating design efforts, I carefully review the information I have gathered to consider all input provided with the goal of considering alternatives that best align with the perceived level of commitment to achieve SaaS governance and optimization results. Was there a recent high-profile renewal that the client feels they were treated poorly and want to regain some leverage or is there a true systemic effort to govern the category? Depending on the trigger, design and ultimate recommendations will vary.

Design

The key deliverable and output of the Assess phase is a basic Strength-Weakness-Opportunity-Threat (SWOT) analysis based on the cumulative learnings of the client contacts interviewed. I make certain to maintain confidentiality of any individual comments, but document the consistent and persistent themes that have emerged. At this point, I am able to get a sense of the likely personality of the emerging SaaS governance and optimization capability and potential conflicts or limiters that could impact the extent of value delivered. Ultimately my wrap-up summarizes a series of recommendations, ultimately producing a roadmap illustrating a recommended SaaS capability evolution, the key milestones and expected outcomes.

I have found there tends to be 3 distinct paths that emerge based upon the insight gained during the assessment phase of the implementation methodology. They are:

- **SaaS Optimization Shared Accountability:** The client recognizes that there is an ongoing SaaS optimization opportunity but it does not warrant or gain the support for a dedicated, new function. While the client may show an interest and willingness to invest in a platform to support optimization efforts of targeted list of SaaS applications used across the organization, the decision is to have vendor management and sourcing assume accountability to document optimization save and cost avoidance.

  Functioning as the SaaS Governance Enabler, I recognize this outcome is not a comprehensive approach that addresses multiple optimization levers and ignores the issues of compliance risk and security vulnerabilities; however, it serves as a point of entry for the activity of SaaS optimization. SaaS Governance Enablers should not become frustrated and continue to use the ESO tools to document and report on SaaS portfolio developments.

- **SaaS Governance Team:** We have spoken of the multi-function, multi-discipline team throughout *The Survival Guide to SaaS Optimization*. Clients tend to move directly to this solution as the out-of-pocket investment is little more than a 'shared accountability' approach but brings together an invaluable group to establish the foundation for true comprehensive, centralized treatment of the SaaS governance and optimization agenda. With proper execution of the ESO framework, SaaS Governance Enablers stand a very high probability this approach will evolve to become a full-time SaaS Optimization Office.

- **SaaS Optimization Office:** When a client has a strong compliance culture, third party risk and a focus on information security, executives are increasingly moving right to the decision to establish a small, dedicated team to address SaaS governance in addition to SaaS optimization. In this scenario, it is essential SaaS Governance Enablers work to reinforce and align expectations as many times executives may have very unrealistic opinions on the time to achieve operational effectiveness and the level of effort necessary to establish the key business unit relationships necessary.

While we have identified the likely approach to SaaS optimization that aligns with a client's appetite and vision, it is also important to take into account the personality type of the client as this will influence the ultimate SaaS governance and optimization solution and must be taken into account during your design efforts.

SaaS Optimization Office: Personality Types

It is important to stress that all of the following SaaS Optimization Office personalities will produce value for an organization in their effort to govern and optimize their SaaS portfolio. SaaS Governance Enablers need to understand internal expectations for the SaaS governance effort in order to build a roadmap that takes the organization from current state to the ultimate long-term SaaS governance and optimization capability. Basically, you need to know where you are starting from and the targeted future state operating model to build the strategy and tactics to reach the destination.

- *'Tool-Centric'*: Currently the majority of clients I work with have a 'tool first' focus for establishing SaaS optimization. Implementation of the SaaS Management

Platform will magically deliver optimization results with little to no support. Just turn it on and you're optimizing!

With this personality, SaaS Governance Enablers need to continually reinforce the need for investment to truly take advantage of the platform's capabilities. This investment could be in terms of ensuring the appropriate diligence and manpower is applied to ensure the tool is fully integrated and the teams have the expertise and time to extract and analyze the data in advance of key decision points.

- *'Part-Timers':* Closely aligned with a Tool-Centric personality, many potential SaaS governance sponsors and stakeholders view SaaS governance and optimization as a part time effort, intended to primarily support Sourcing's efforts to deliver optimized renewals. Much of what I have shared in *The Survival Guide to SaaS Optimization* and the ESO framework can be applied by SaaS Governance Enablers to influence these sponsors and stakeholders over time to see the value in a dedicated, ongoing effort.

  This SaaS governance personality type is closely aligned to the 'Tool-centric' personality with a narrow definition of governance and optimization. The strategy for SaaS Governance Enablers is to continually report the value delivered utilizing the core tools of the ESO framework and in time the view of optimization will broaden.

- *'Finance-Fixated':* Much of the challenge today faced by organizations is effective measurement of total SaaS spend and assignment of this spend to the appropriate business unit and cost center. Applying the ESO framework, SaaS Governance Enablers have worked closely with IT finance to identify the reporting and analysis that will support budget and forecast requirements. I have found close alignment between SaaS governance and optimization efforts with IT finance produces a strong base on which SaaS Governance Enablers can expand their efforts.

- *'Risk-Anxiety':* This is a high-growth SaaS governance and optimization personality type that has emerged significantly over the past year. Interestingly, what I continue to find is leaders of Third Party Risk Management and Governance, Risk and Compliance are strategic targets for SaaS Management Platform providers, yet the platforms today offer no real risk monitoring or vulnerability capability. As this dynamic becomes more visible to TPRM and GRC tool providers, I anticipate their platforms will begin to add modules to support some basic SaaS governance and optimization requirements. Currently this is not the case so SaaS Governance Enablers need to consider close alignment with existing TPRM or GRC platforms, adopting their definitions and categorization structure into Tool 5 of the ESO framework, SaaS Risk Categorization.

When I am engaged by a client with a strong compliance and Information Security focus, I have found sponsors and stakeholders view optimization in a broader context and accelerate the move to a standing SaaS Governance Team model or perhaps even move directly to a dedicated SaaS Optimization Office. The determining factors tend to be the size and diversity of the SaaS portfolio, if there was a recent exploited security vulnerability or an inquiry from regulators has raised visibility on SaaS implications.

When I find a client in this personality type, I put ESO framework Tool 5, SaaS Risk Categorization front and center. Demonstrating an awareness of the challenges encountered by TPRM, GRC and InfoSec leaders and the ability of a SaaS governance investment to support and extend their ability to identify emerging risk prior to impact.

- SaaS Optimization Office Platform Alignment

During the Assessment phase of the ESO Implementation methodology, you will get a sense as to the desire of sponsors and stakeholders' willingness to invest in a SaaS Management Platform to support governance and optimization efforts. I typically observe 3 outcomes on this topic with each presenting a challenge to SaaS Governance Enablers. However, I have found proactive measures to establish realistic expectations with executive sponsors and stakeholders will in time, support adoption of a SaaS Management Platform with the appropriate levels of integration and necessary staff to generate strong governance and optimization outcomes.

o **SaaS Portal Strategy:** If your organizations SaaS portfolio is not viewed as large enough to warrant an investment in staff or dedicated platform, SaaS Governance Enablers can prioritize SaaS partners using the output from the Empowered SaaS Optimization framework tools. Based on the selected criteria and renewal timing, license usage and type management intelligence can be extracted from the specific SaaS partners portal or tenant. This approach, however, does not address monitoring or assessing risk introduced to operations by SaaS partners.

o **Stand-alone SaaS Platform:** In some respects, this is a 'back-room' approach to SaaS optimization as there is limited visibility or interaction across the other functions and disciplines who benefit from a comprehensive approach to SaaS governance and optimization efforts. Currently, I observe the vast majority of tool deployments fit this category. When combined with an appropriate back-office staff, this style of implementation provides strong governance and optimization results across a large portion of the SaaS portfolio.

o **Integrated SaaS Platform:** There has been a

significant trend for compliance, security and risk professionals to be engaged in the discussions to establish SaaS governance and optimization capabilities. I find these organizations will quickly focus on establishing SaaS Management Platform integration across purchasing and other channels by which assets are procured as well as compliance, risk and security platforms. In this scenario, Tool 5, SaaS Risk Categorization, is a great platform to establish alignment with these critical functional areas and extend the value delivered by the SaaS Management Platform.

In each of these SaaS Management Platform Alignment scenarios, during the Design phase, SaaS Governance Enablers can use Tool 2, SaaS Control Map, Tool 7, SaaS Optimization Levers and Tool 4, SaaS Optimization Decomposition, to craft high level requirements for the SaaS Management Platform and initiate the evaluation and selection process. During this process, be certain to tie the recommendations with SWOT findings and educate executive sponsors and stakeholders of the expected results.

Implement

With Design completed based on the output of the Assessment phase, SaaS Governance Enablers will present to sponsors and stakeholders the detailed recommendations for establishing the SaaS governance capability. Typically, this occurs as some sort of executive committee meeting at which time approval to proceed is granted and the model endorsed. During this session, I have found it important to emphasize with executive sponsors how the recommendation supports the current SaaS portfolio and the manner in which it will evolve and mature as expectations change and SaaS portfolio composition change. We need to make certain it is understood we are governing and optimizing a rapidly growing and diversifying group of partners and capabilities.

- **Front-Office Implementation:** There is a small, subtle movement for executives to invest in a dedicated SaaS resource to function as the face of SaaS governance and optimization. This trend is most evident in organizations whose view of governance and optimization includes both spend efficiency and risk monitoring and I believe it will continue to grow. However, the majority of implementations today is for the Sourcing IT Category Manager to be assigned the task of SaaS optimization. In this scenario, utilizing the assets of the Empowered SaaS Optimization framework will enable you to continually document the importance of effective SaaS governance and the value to be realized by an expanded effort.

- **Scope Addition:** Typical functions who will be tapped to lead the SaaS governance and optimization effort are Sourcing and Vendor Management leaders with the focus being effective renewal support. Application of the ESO framework will support these teams in their effort to quantify the SaaS portfolio, establish the needed policies and controls and align activities across the SaaS Governance Framework to deliver effective SaaS renewal outcomes.

- **Dedicated SaaS Leaders:** I have found the decision to create a dedicated, net-new function is typically made by an organization whose leaders are attune to the extent of the governance and optimization challenge or are focused on third party risk measures and security vulnerabilities. This represents a small percent today, but I continue to see evidence that firms will invest in a full-time dedicated SaaS governance and optimization when executives are properly informed and educated on the dual-value aspects of spend management and risk identification and mitigation.

- **Back-Office Implementation:** During the Design phase, SaaS Governance Enablers will typically focus on selection of a tool and the manpower needed to execute the targeted SaaS optimization activities. What I have observed as an all-too common outcome is the executive steering committee, sponsors and stakeholders eliminate the staffing investment, instead relying on the capability of the tool to deliver the targeted optimization results.

  I believe the root cause of this outcome is the tendency of tool account teams to overstate capability and understate the need for staff and integration efforts. Combined with the exuberance of SaaS Governance Enablers to highlight the value the tool will bring to optimization efforts, sponsors and stakeholders make the very natural conclusion based on the information provided.

- **Scope Addition:** Expectations for the effectiveness for Back-Office activities assigned to current staff, typically in Sourcing or Vendor Management, need to be carefully managed. Utilize ESO Tool 7 and Tool 1, Optimization Levers by Segment and SaaS Active Universe Roster, to prioritize and focus activities. Make certain individuals who will be assuming the task of SaaS optimization receive appropriate training in the SaaS Management Platform and are coached on how to extract license usage data from the assigned SaaS partner portals.

- **Dedicated SaaS Analyst:** With the investment in a proper team of analyst, SaaS governance and optimization efforts can extend beyond Lever 1 and Lever 2 usage optimization to include risk monitoring and due diligence activities.

SaaS Governance Enablers need to be flexible, understanding that where we start is not ultimately where we want to stay. Utilize the ESO framework tools to continually educate and inform sponsors and stakeholders on the additional opportunities to achieve spend efficiency with managed risk, highlighting the natural benefits achieved as operations mature and the SaaS portfolio expands.

Operational Maturation

Throughout *The Survival Guide to SaaS Optimization* I have spoken about the evolutionary nature of an organizations approach to the activity of SaaS governance and optimization. Throughout the process of implementing the ESO framework, it is essential SaaS Governance Enablers continually reinforce the ultimate vision for a comprehensive SaaS Optimization Office that delivers SaaS spend efficiency, reduced security vulnerabilities as well as risk and compliance management.

- **SaaS Optimization Office Operational Maturation:** A technique I use to help executive sponsors visualize where their SaaS governance and optimization capabilities are and where they will ultimately achieve is to produce a time line or scale that illustrates where they are on the spectrum of SaaS operations. I will typically show this type of image during the design and implementation phases of the methodology in order to help executives see exactly where the recommended operation is placed relative to all potential alternatives. Now that implementation has been accomplished, it is important to reinforce with these same individuals the activities underway to mature operations and the benefits to be realized.

  - **SaaS G&O Evolution Phases:** I like to have the broad SaaS governance optimization phases we have described throughout *The Survival Guide to SaaS Optimization* as the header of the visual. Directly

Empowered SaaS Optimization - Tool 9
SaaS Governance & Optimization Maturation Map
Current State / Target State Review <DATE>

SaaS G&O Evolutionary Phase	SaaS Governance Enabler			SaaS Governance Team			SaaS Optimization Office			
SaaS G&O Effectiveness Scale	1	2	3	4	5	6	7	8	9	10
Current State Effectiveness Assessment		◯								
SaaS G&O Target State Effectiveness							◯			
Phase Characteristics / Core Activities	Centralized SaaS Universe			Defined SaaS Policies & Controls			Dedicated Staff executing FO & BO activities			
	SaaS Spend Analysis			Defined SaaS Control Map			Internal Process Alignment			
	Preliminary SaaS Segmentation			Renewal Map			SaaS Risk Categorization Fully defined and aligned with TRPM/GRC			
	Partial Implementation of Optimization Levers 1 & 2			SaaS Management Platform			Full Implementation of Optimization Levers 1,2,3,4,5			
	Preliminary SaaS Policies & Controls			Full Implementation of Optimization Levers 1 & 2			Implmentation of SaaS Strategic Partner Program			
	SaaS Governance Enablers report/inform targedted Executive Sponsors			Broadening of SaaS Optimization emerging			Business Unit alignment with documented value delivered			
	CURRENT PERIOD ACTIVITIES						UPCOMING PERIOD ACTIVITIES			

SaaS Governance & Optimization Maturity Map

below I have two separate indicators. One for 'Current State', the second for 'Target State'.

o **SaaS G&O Effectiveness Scale:** I have found establishing an alignment of the 3 SaaS governance and optimization phases with a simple scale of 1 – 10 helps executives quickly see the value they will realize based upon the investment made.

o **Current State Effectiveness Assessment:** As the leader or SaaS Governance Enabler, this is the opportunity to self-assess current performance using the SaaS Phase Characteristics as the guide.

o **SaaS G&O Target State Effectiveness:** An additional visual that is very powerful in showing the expected level of SaaS governance and effectiveness based on the level of support and investment from executive sponsors. If the team has stopped short of forming a SaaS Governance Team, I will slide the indicator to align with 3 on the SaaS G&O Effectiveness Scale. If executive sponsors have supported formation of the SaaS Governance Team but stopped short of investing in a dedicated team, I slide the indicator to 6. If the executive sponsors have invested in the dedicated SaaS Optimization Office with full time front-office and back-office capabilities, I will slide the indicator to 9 or 10 depending on the level of interaction with risk, compliance and security leadership.

o **Phase Characteristics / Core Activities:** Utilizing the Empowered SaaS Optimization framework, I insert a brief summary of the key operational elements and benefits achieved by the specific SaaS evolutionary phase. This again helps me reinforce with the executives the expected benefit they will realize for the level of investment.

- o **Current Period Activities:** I populate a brief listing of the primary activities the team is currently implementing and stabilizing.

- o **Upcoming Period Activities:** A brief summary of the task, activities and perhaps the ESO tools to be implemented in the coming quarter.

Tool 9, SaaS Governance and Optimization Operational Maturation Map is an approach I highly recommend SaaS Governance Enablers take the time to create and utilize frequently with executive sponsors and stakeholders to continually reinforce what has been accomplished to date, current operational capabilities and the upcoming benefits to be realized with the next targeted activities. When I have been asked by clients to assess their current SaaS governance and optimization maturity, I do use the template for Tool 9 as the basis and add a few additional criteria from the ESO framework tools. This has proven successful as the output will help reinforce current state aligned with the ultimate targeted operations.

Part 5 Closure: ESO Framework Methodology Implementation

In Part 5, I have attempted to provide insight to the methodology I employ when implementing the Empowered SaaS Optimization framework with a client. Much of what I describe deals with establishing and managing expectations of executive sponsors and stakeholders and keeping them grounded as the SaaS governance and optimization capability stabilizes and becomes operational. This is best accomplished by continually updating and revising the content contained within the ESO tools and presenting the summary in a clean, powerful fashion.

SaaS Governance Enabler Outlook

We have reached the end of *The Survival Guide to SaaS Optimization* but only the beginning of an exciting career opportunity. Thank you for taking the time to learn about the Empowered SaaS Optimization framework and each of the individual tools designed to help you take on the role of SaaS Governance Enabler and help your organization see the value in establishing a comprehensive SaaS governance and optimization operation.

By applying the ESO framework and the insight provided, you will be well positioned in this high growth, high visibility segment. As SaaS applications become increasingly embedded in core enterprise services, the need for organizations to manage these assets will become a top priority for corporate executives. With leading consultancies such as Gartner continually documenting the importance to govern and optimize SaaS assets, there is little doubt that SaaS governance and optimization will emerge as an important function, establishing a net-new career path for those of you who choose to invest the time to understand the implications of SaaS services on your organization's operations.

As the SaaS Governance Enabler, I offer a few last words of advice intended to help you regardless of the current level of focus your organization has on SaaS governance and optimization today.

- Focus your energies on being a facilitator, driving collaboration across the disciplines and functions that contribute to development of a comprehensive SaaS governance and optimization capability.

- Understand the unique perspective and needs of each of these areas and look for areas of common interest.

- Continually engage business unit leaders to understand their goals, objectives and needs. Being viewed as an enabler by these individuals is a key determinant to SaaS governance and optimization success.

- Become expert in the tools and platforms used by the various teams to understand their contribution and how SaaS can support, align and extend identification and monitoring of third parties and risk.

- Take full advantage of the Empowered SaaS Optimization framework to create the transparency necessary for executive leadership to fully appreciate the extent of the current SaaS portfolio and forecasted growth across the enterprise.

- Utilize the initial versions of the ESO templates you created to keep track of progress.

- Be patient and remain focused, in time, you will be well positioned when the opportunity emerges.

Good Luck in your SaaS Governance & Optimization career. I look forward to supporting your efforts to deliver outstanding value to your organization.

Jim

List of Acronyms

API	Application Programming Interface
BAU	Business As Usual
CCO	Chief Compliance Officer
CCOE	Cloud Center of Excellence
CEO	Chief Executive Officer
CFO	Chief Financial Officer
CIO	Chief Information Officer
CISO	Chief Information Security Officer
D&O	Deliverables and Obligations
ESO	Empowered SaaS Optimization
Exec SteerCo	Executive Steering Committee
FLOD	First Line of Defense
GDPR	General Data Protection Regulation
GRC	Governance, Risk and Compliance
HCM	Human Capital Management
IA	Internal Audit
IA	Intelligent Automation
IaaS	Infrastructure as a Service
InfoSec	Information Security
ISV	Independent Software Vendors
IT	Information Technology
KLO	Keep the Lights On
PaaS	Platform as a Service
PII	Personally Identifiable Information
POC	Proof of Concept
RACI	Responsible-Accountable-Consult-Inform
RFI	Request for Information
RFP	Request for Proposal
RoE	Rules of Engagement
SaaS	Software as a Service
SAM	Software Asset Management
SGT	SaaS Governance Team
SLA	Service Level Agreement
SLOD	Second Line of Defense
SOO	SaaS Optimization Office
SSO	Single Sign On
SWOT	Strength-Weakness-Opportunity-Threat
TEM	Telecom Expense Management
TLOD	Third Line of Defense
TPRM	Third Party Risk Management
VMO	Vendor Management Office

About the Author

Jim Hussey is the former leader of a Fortune 500 technology vendor management organization. In this role, he was responsible for Software Asset Management, Telecom Expense Management, IT First Line of Defense (FLOD) Third Party Risk Management and IT Sourced Services. In addition, working closely with his IT sourcing partner and Chief Procurement Officer, Jim led the development of the Policies and Controls for utilization of Software as a Service capabilities in addition to the detailed requirements workflow by which use of a SaaS application would be approved.

The Survival Guide to SaaS Optimization is Jim's follow-up effort to the *The SAM Leader Survival Guide*. Through the combination of his experience supporting clients establish SaaS governance operations, extensive interviews with corporate executives, leaders of SaaS Management Platform providers and his corporate role establishing a SaaS Governance and Optimization function, Jim has created the Empowered SaaS Optimization framework as a means to help interested professionals develop and apply SaaS governance and optimization best practices, positioning their careers in this high-growth segment.

Jim is a frequent featured speaker on the subjects of Software Asset Management, Third Party Risk Management and SaaS Governance and Optimization best practices. Utilizing his background in research and journalism, he continues to work with leading associations to produce insightful research on these subjects with the goal of continually providing valuable insight to assist professionals achieved greater career success.

Jim is currently the leader of NPI's SAM and SaaS Optimization practice.

Lightning Source UK Ltd.
Milton Keynes UK
UKHW011919020421
381444UK00001B/34